THIS MAGIC MOMENT

Musical Reflections of a Generation

Harry Turner

A G M Enterprises, Incorporated
Atlanta, Georgia

FIRST EDITION

Cover design by Cheri Wenger Designs
Editor-in-chief Jean French

Library of Congress Catalog Card Number: 94-70572

ISBN 0-9640761-0-1 (hardbound)
ISBN 0-9640761-1-X (paperbound)

To you, the great artists,
the creators of America's golden music.
My fondest wish is that this book
may give to you as much joy
as your music has brought to me
and millions of other fans.
That it will tell those that aren't aware,
wherein lives the true heart of rock and roll!

CONTENTS

ACKNOWLEDGMENTS

I am deeply indebted to those who have believed in what the music, the message and this book is all about. People like William Abram, Frank Aldridge, Frank Allen, Harold Anderson, William Andrews, Bobby Barber, William Bell, Joan Black, Duncan Bowers, Richard Brassell, Tony Brooks, Randy Brunson, Don Bryant, Jim Buie, Dr. Ed Byrd, Jerry Calvert, Mike Campbell, Ken Chapman, Steve Charles, Ken Chastain, Olivia Cloud, Stan Darden, Jim Davis, Jerry DuBose, Eloise Dukes, Kathy Dukes, Granville Elliott, Arthur Epps, Tad Fogle, Eugene Frazier, Sapp Funderburk, Nancy Ghertner, Jimmy Gibbs, Pete Gilyard, Jeff Gluck, Leighton Grantham, Jim Green, Bob Gregory, Merwin Gross, Judith Haimes, Tom Harrell, Eugene Harris, Ron Harris, Jim Hartley, John Huffstetler, Richard Hunt, Paula Hunter, Obie Jessie, Eugene Jessup, Chuck Johnson, Frederick S. Jones, Jean E. Jones, Phil Kehr, Dr. Henry Kelley, Marilyn Kelley, Frank King, Jack Lang, Darryl Lassiter, Finn Lawritsen, Joab Lesesne, Jr., Dell Long, Earle Mauldin, Larry McGehee, Mike MacMillan, Earle Morris, Betty Mojjis, John Mojjis, Rodney Moss, Max Oates, Brett O'Hara, Cyndee Parker, Ernie Payne, Joe Pinner, Coach Tom Pucci, John Rampey, Darrell Ray, Gene Reeves, Ron Rich, Rik Rogers, Nancy Ross, Bill Rush, Beau Sanders, Norris Scoggins, Billy Scott, Walter Scott, John Seymour, Hugh Simpson, George Smith, Miles Smith, Kaj Sorensen, Thomas E. Stewart, Allan Strait, Eugene Stuckey, Talmadge Stuckey, Frank Suggs, Roy Swancy, Jim Taylor, Roy Tuck, Tony Union, David Vaughn, Richard Verciglio, Dennis Waldrop, Robert Waldrop, Dave Welchel—who encouraged, advised or helped these efforts.

To my children Erin, Harmon and Anna and grandson Zachary. To my sister Aubrey, half-sisters Allison, Bootsie, Beth and Dottie, and members of the extended Turner and Allen families. To my wife's family, Sid and Irene Moorhead, Sid Moorhead, Jr., Leslie and Pamela French. Finally, to my mother Carol, my father Harry and my step-father Stokes who are deceased, and my step-mother Betty—whose guidance and influence helped shape my life's perspectives and values.

But none of this would have been possible without the sweat and sacrifice for—and unshakable belief in both me and the book-of my wife, Jean. I'm not sure I can ever fully express my gratitude and love!

INTRODUCTION

The book you have in front of you expresses my personal reflections about a special music and the lasting influences of music on society in general. However, the music of which I write suffers from the lack of a universally recognized name. It encompasses good-time rock and roll, rhythm and blues, doo-wop, Motown, New Orleans music, blues, rockabilly, Carolina beach music, shag music, soul music, the Memphis/Muscle Shoals sound, the sound of Chicago, the sound of Philadelphia, California surf music, and Texas boogie-blues. Collectively, the term broadly defines what was known as American rock and roll before the definition was altered by the British music invasion of the mid-60's. It does not consist of: British rock, folk music, folk rock, hard rock, country and western, rap, hip hop, heavy metal, teen idol music, Broadway/Hollywood mainstream pop, or jazz.

Other American music types have identifiable geographical centers. Broadway/Hollywood mainstream popular music is linked to New York due to Broadway and Tin Pan Alley; and Hollywood, California with its great Hollywood musicals. Country and western has its roots in Nashville, Tennessee with the Grand Ole Opry and the city's recording industry, while jazz is synonymous with New Orleans and its vibrant Dixieland jazz traditions. The music of which I write has many separate geographical ties to places like Detroit, Chicago, Cleveland, New York, Memphis, Muscle Shoals, Los Angeles and Philadelphia. There has never been a concentrated power base for this music which a recognized geographical tie would have afforded.

This music is an original American art form, and is unique to the American experience but it has been saddled with a confusing jumble of monikers: oldies, oldies but goodies, moldy oldies, 50's music, 60's music, 50's and 60's music, sock hop music, good-time rock and roll, doo-wop, soul music, Motown, beach music, golden oldies, and others. With these disparate names it is no wonder that the music's very identification has been so fragmented. To make matters worse, the use of the term "oldies" is the kiss of death in our modern, youth-crazed society. It's noteworthy that the older recordings of British-influenced rock and roll have been given the easier, more explanatory, and more dignified description—classic rock.

This much loved music will now be classified to readers by a much easier, certainly more dignified, more accurate, more respectful, and more honestly reflective description: **America's golden music.**

Harry Turner

CHAPTER 1

A FIRST TASTE OF SOULFUL MUSIC

There was a golden time when music gave a depth of meaning to our lives and could move us as a nation. The proud creators of America's rock and roll and rhythm and blues (R&B), whom I have come to know and love, literally forged the soundtrack for so many of our lives. Yet they have been taken for granted, ignored, even forgotten. There was an honesty and innocence to their music that was a reflection of kinder, gentler times. It is both sad and regrettable that the very essence of those magical days is missing, and tragically, we are all victims of that loss, especially our children.

It's time to set the record straight about what really happened to America's golden music and a simpler, saner time; how the British music invasion stole from its originators, pushed them aside and set in motion forces that altered the very fabric of society.

The special times they created will be remembered and they will be honored for the tremendous contributions they have made. Their delightful, heartfelt music will be given back to a society that can use a healthy dose of uncompromising, fun-filled entertainment. Those days are about to begin again as I relate my lifelong love affair with the music.

Luck surely played in my favor regarding the time of my birth. To have grown up during the wondrous years while rock and roll music was inventing itself is something I'm ever grateful for. Music, rock and roll of the 50's and 60's in particular, has been a big part of my life since childhood. The only element to equal this good fortune has been to befriend and work with so many of the artists who have made the music I have enjoyed since my youth. As rock and roll symbolizes the hope of the

1

human spirit, so childhood personifies that hope.

In the late 40's my sister, Aubrey and I, were living with our mother in Greenville, S.C. Because mother worked, our housekeeper Dora greeted us after school. Occasionally, Dora took us to her home. Being at Dora's gave Aubrey and me a wonderful feeling as we were treated very warmly by her family and her neighbors. And it was at Dora's where I began to experience my first taste of "soulful" music, especially Negro spirituals, which were so full of life and good feelings. This was the beginning of the influence of black music on my life.

Our mother, Carol, was the third child born to Basil and Eulalah Allen—Doc and Mom to us. Doc was a dentist and Mom the dutiful housewife. They lived in a cozy two story house on shady, tree-lined Clarendon Avenue, north of Greenville. Mom was without a doubt the best cook who ever lived. My mouth still waters today for her delicious boiled custard.

Doc and Mom were a good case in support of the old saying "opposites attract." Mom was the walking definition of a lady; Doc on the other hand, was an out-and-out character. While Mom had to stretch to reach five feet, Doc was a very large, barrel-chested man. Mom was a loyal member of Central Baptist Church, and Doc was equally loyal in his non-attendance. During prohibition he and some doctor friends supposedly drove up to the mountains of North Carolina for bootleg whiskey. Yet at the same time, Doc was extremely well-read and was quite an authority on Abraham Lincoln, and won many a ribbon for his prized roses that he grew in his garden. But I used to wonder why, if he were the ruler of the roost, he had to go out to the garage behind the house whenever he wanted a sip of his favorite bourbon.

Mother was the cute, precocious little sister to older brothers, Richard and Severn. She was very popular during her school days, but not conceited, which was a rare combination among the high school crowd. She didn't alter these traits as an adult; she had a winsome personality and loved to have a good time, but never ran with the crowd except on her terms. She refused to go to meetings such as P.T.A., passing them off as "so much baloney." My penchant for non-conformity came naturally, as she was a total individualist.

The Allen family had a deep fondness for music. Doc instilled in me an appreciation of classical and semi-classical music. We listened to

2

the Gilbert and Sullivan Operetta, "H.M.S. Pinafore" on more than one occasion. Uncle Richard, Uncle Severn and mother all loved the big band sound. They were great fans of artists like Glenn Miller, the Dorsey Brothers, Benny Goodman, Louis Armstrong, Bing Crosby, Ella Fitzgerald, Harry James, Artie Shaw, Guy Lombardo, and Frank Sinatra.

Almost all of the popular songs that I enjoyed had that good-time feeling. What happy times can be remembered with: "I'm Looking Over A Four Leaf Clover" by Art Mooney, "The Woody Woodpecker Song" by Kay Kyser, "Goodnight Irene," and "On Top Of Ole Smokey" by the Weavers, "Down Yonder" by Del Wood, "I Get So Lonely" by the Four Knights, "Mockingbird Hill" and the beautiful "Tennessee Waltz" by Patti Page.

It was probably unusual for a kid my age, but our marching to and from classes at Miss Haynesworth's Private School led me to a love of the march music of John Phillip Sousa. The use of multiple snare drums provided me with an appreciation of the snare drum beat which was to become "the big beat" of rhythm and blues and rock and roll.

Daddy (his first name was Harry) lived in Ware Shoals, S.C. He was divorced from Mother but we were with him almost every weekend. Daddy was an avid music fan, especially of the big band sound, and he was also quite an accomplished dancer and could really "cut the rug," as the saying goes. He won many a jitterbug contest, and even when he was much older, people would approach him in public and turn to Aubrey and me to tell us what a great dancer he was. He had quite an extensive record collection and I often accompanied him on his record buying forays to Payne's For Music in Greenville. With this constant exposure to record collecting it seems my fate was sealed. It wasn't long before I began my own collection, with no way to fathom how vital a part of my life it would become. Daddy often took Aubrey and me to movies, horseback riding, to ball games and such. But my favorite pastime was riding in his black Studebaker convertible with the top down, listening to music on the radio.

Although Daddy dated several ladies, there was never one quite like Betty Partee. She was a student nurse at the Greenville Hospital School of Nursing, and I thought she was beautiful. Evidently Daddy thought so too, as they decided to marry. The wedding took place at the Buncombe Street Methodist Church in Greenville and was quite the

3

event.

Their first home was the Ware Shoals Inn. The formal dining room, with tables dressed in starched white cloths, always carried the tempting aroma of freshly baked breads and cakes. Daddy had a huge radio-turntable unit and frequently played his records allowing me to do so as well, as long as I was very careful. My particular favorites in his collection were the fun, up-tempo numbers, mainly the good-time piano music of Frankie Carle and various Dixieland platters. "Play A Simple Melody" by Bing Crosby and his son Gary was one song I loved to sing along to.

After Daddy and Betty bought a home, almost every weekend they had friends over for cookouts in the sprawling back-yard. They'd play horseshoes and ping pong, and belt-out their favorite songs. The strains of Daddy, along with Earle Mauldin, Grace Hartman and other friends singing the Mills Brothers' hit "Up A Lazy River" (though granted, not quite as harmoniously as brothers Herbert, Harry, Donald and John Mills) still rings clear in my ears.

Daddy also enjoyed some of the R&B music (called "race" music at the time by the music industry) that was available on jukeboxes in restaurants. One little eatery in Ware Shoals had several records by an artist named Piano Red who played boogie woogie piano. Two jumping numbers that I liked were "Rockin' With Red" and "Red's Boogie." Piano Red, whose real name was Willie Perryman, was a radio disc jockey (DJ) in Atlanta. [He performed frequently on college campuses and had quite a following. In 1962 he changed his name to Dr. Feelgood and had two national hits in "Dr. Feelgood" and "The Right String But The Wrong Yo Yo". I saw him perform in person only once—at Muhlenbrink's Saloon in Underground Atlanta in the 70's. He was still fantastic and I purchased an album from him on the spot].

Daddy's love for Piano Red's music helped form my music taste, but I'm not sure that he was ever aware of the fact. My affinity for boogie woogie, honky tonk, barrelhouse, spiritual, and gospel revival piano styles had been spawned by then and Piano Red's music personified a lot of it for me. My father and Betty's love and enjoyment of music also provided me with a strong and lasting influence as to the role music plays in special times among good friends.

We also spent many weekends with Daddy's parents, Tom and

4

Ruth Turner—Granddaddy and Nana to us—at their home in Greenville. Granddaddy died when I was only seven years old, but I still remember him making the best homemade pancakes I ever tasted. Nana worked at the Glendale, one of Greenville's finest ladies' clothing stores. Whenever any of us grandkids would visit she would always slip money to us as a treat. She was a very wise lady and I really admired her.

An annual event that many members of the extended Turner family attended was "Camp Meeting." Since 1832 (except during the four years of the Civil War) this took place—and still does-each August for a span of ten days at Poplar Springs Methodist Campground, located between Royston and Lavonia, Georgia. The wooded camp grounds were comprised of simple wooden cabins which surrounded a shady, open church arbor. Each cabin was much like a barn stall and had a sawdust floor. The sawdust had a nice, clean smell and, since we were often barefoot, it usually got stuck between our toes. We had to be discreet in our night-wear as we could easily see from room to room. And we had to find our way to the rickety, old outhouses in the pitch dark, tripping over tree stumps and such. The scary, black pits were full of spider webs and bugs, much to the girls' horror. To us kids, though, it was a magical place, and part of the appeal was that it was so unlike home.

Granddaddy was up before daylight to stoke the wood stove for the day's food preparations. The smell of wood smoke and frying chicken wafted throughout the campground and gave us all a fierce appetite. None of us kids ever needed a dinner bell! Aubrey, cousins Tommy, Buddy, Eddie and I got to ride on the horse-drawn wagons that delivered ice for the cabins, which was both fun and work, as we helped carry the ice. We were allowed to go to "the stand" to get candy, snow cones, and drinks with the nickels and dimes we had saved from home. And we played penny ante poker with match sticks until late at night, way after our regular bed-time. We did the things that kids liked to do in the summertime; we hunted for "buckeyes" during the day and fire-flies at night, we played "follow the leader," we hiked until we were sore, and swam in the freezing cold water at Chick Springs to cool off. And we guys all had crushes on the beautiful Shirley girls, Ann, Rosemary, and Sue, who stayed in the next cabin.

The open church, standing tall and proud with its massive beams, held rows of sturdy wooden pews and an altar. Services were held three times a day and family members attended every time the conch shell sounded the call. The music consisted mainly of beautiful, melodious and upbeat revival hymns such as "Dwelling In Beulah Land," "Standing On The Promises," "Power In The Blood," "In My Heart There Rings A Melody" and "Love Lifted Me." There was always a choir and the only accompaniment was an old, upright piano. My great aunt Lura Bruce was one of the pianists and it made me so proud when she would literally bang the piano as we sang along. This only deepened my love for good-time piano music.

Occasionally I sang in the choir. During one hymn, I got carried away by the music and was singing so loudly that a member of the congregation, Colonel Cheek, abruptly stopped the service and offered to donate $100 if I would sing a solo. Although I was scared senseless, I rustled up my nerve, and actually enjoyed the experience. This was my first moment in the spotlight, and my first glimpse of the intimate relationship between performer and audience.

Occasionally, I still go to camp meeting, but find that, sadly, as an adult, it does not hold quite the same charm as it did for me as a child. Nevertheless, there is still a stirring in my soul when I enter the wooded area surrounding Poplar Springs, and the piano and chorus again resound with such spirit and fervor in my mind.

Dora retired and was succeeded by Pearl Coleman. She too had a deep influence on my love for music. At times Pearl would baby-sit at night, and when she did, she never missed her favorite radio show, "The Meeting House In Dixie." It was broadcast live from a black church and consisted mainly of up-tempo spiritual music. Much like the music I had heard at Dora's, I loved it because of its happy, unrestrained nature. Pearl was both amused and pleased that I enjoyed listening with her, because she had evidently never been around a little white boy so thoroughly mesmerized by the music. It was a special thing between us. At Pearl's, I became acquainted with an extraordinary, fiery, deeply soulful voice—it belonged to gospel singer Mahalia Jackson.

Pearl and I also shared an enjoyment of R&B as did many of my schoolmates. While walking to and from school, my friends and I would sing at the top of our lungs—mostly off-key—the words to some of our favorite rhythm and blues records such as, "Drinking Wine Spo-Dee-O-Dee" by Stick McGhee and "Stack-O-Lee" by Archibald. By this time artists like Louis Jordan and his Tympany 5, Amos Milburn, the Ravens, Ruth Brown, the Orioles, the Clovers, Charles Brown, Champion Jack Dupree, Joe Turner, the Dominoes, Wynonie Harris, Professor Longhair, and even Fats Domino were already on the scene, but as yet I had not discovered them. My unique education was continuing to broaden.

CHAPTER 2

FROM BIG BAND TO ROCK AND ROLL

While I was in my formative stages, as far as musical tastes were concerned, popular music itself was on the verge of a big change. During the 30's and 40's, the big band sound had dominated the scene. Big band music was a white man's music that fused various black music forms including jazz, Dixieland jazz, be-bop, boogie woogie and ragtime among others. There were a few black stars in big band music, but most were white. Even as early as eight years of age, my affinity was for such big band entertainers as Louis Armstrong, Lionel Hampton, Count Basie, Duke Ellington, Pearl Bailey, Ella Fitzgerald, the Mills Brothers, the Ink Spots, Cab Calloway, Billy Eckstine, and Louis Jordan.

These artists had a special soulfulness in their musical presentations that other artists didn't have. And even though my parents would talk about Bing Crosby, Frank Sinatra, and other such artists, they seemed to get the greatest amount of pleasure from the music of black artists when they heard them on the radio or listened to records.

White artists had pretty much dominated the big band sound, even though the style was largely originated by black musicians. This was not unique to the big band era but has gone on throughout recording history. There was even an outcry when black-influenced Dixieland and swing were gaining popularity in the 20's and 30's because discrimination was in full flourish during those years.

In jazz great Lionel Hampton's autobiography, **Hamp,** he states that until he joined Benny Goodman's band, bands were almost entirely segregated by race but that white and black musicians often "jammed" together at after hours clubs for the sheer enjoyment of it. Even so, there was a certain sophistication in music of Hamp's type, and a good per-

8

centage of the blacks playing it were fairly well educated. Some were even college or music school graduates. And to increase record sales and bookings potential, many blacks moderated or "whitened" their music. As a result, society had a certain amount of respect for black jazz and swing.

By this time I had become much in sympathy with blacks because of what my mind perceived to be unfair treatment by society. I recall going with Daddy to a poorer section behind Nana and Grandaddy's house and giving money to some of the black children that lived there. Still, there were those who said that blacks were inferior and did not deserve to be treated as equals. I simply could not understand why the very people who were always so nice to me and with whom I had such good times, deserved such treatment. I was shocked when I realized they had to use separate restaurants, rest rooms, water fountains, swimming pools, and were required to sit in the back of buses. Naively, I had thought that the "white" sign over the entrance to the Ware Shoals bus terminal was advertising a product or something similar—and I simply didn't realize that it meant only white people could enter there. I recall telling a black lady named Nora, who was visiting relatives in Ware Shoals, that someday I was going to do something to help right that wrong. It may have been the vow of an innocent child, but it wasn't offered lightly, nor has it ever been forgotten.

As the big band era was dominated by older artists and the music was somewhat stiff and laid back by teenage standards, there was a void to be filled. By the late 40's and early 50's, teenagers had become a strong marketable force. The time was ripe for something new to capture the restive spirit and rapt attention of newly enfranchised teens, who had spendable incomes—something that was "their own thing." And like most of my friends, I just couldn't wait to turn thirteen!

Quite by accident the teens' "own thing" began to emerge when a DJ in Cleveland, Ohio named Alan Freed began setting the air waves afire with his radio show, "The Moon Dog Show." Freed's concept was to play R&B for blacks. Ironically, young white teenagers were tuning in, and it became the hottest radio show in Cleveland—the numbers of listeners grew like a tent revival.

Freed also began presenting live concerts featuring some of the

9

R&B acts whose records he played. If there was one occasion which probably marked the birth of rock and roll, it was Alan Freed's Moondog Coronation Ball—considered to be the first rock and roll concert. It took place on March 21, 1952 at the Cleveland Arena. Guest artists included Paul Williams, Tiny Grimes, The Dominoes, Danny Cobb, Varetta Dillard and "many others." Advance tickets were $1.50, or $1.75 at the door. The throngs who attended the Coronation Ball were black, but teens like me were beginning to catch the infectious spirit of the music.

As the word spread, so too did Alan's fame—throughout the U.S. He was offered and accepted a DJ slot with WINS radio in New York City in 1954. Alan Freed was truly on his way. From there he propelled the music to new heights by reaching a mammoth white teenage audience. Freed took credit for coining the phrase "rock and roll," which was black street slang for making love. But I well remember Aubrey and I listening to the words in the Dominoes' "Sixty Minute Man," which was a hit in 1951, singing about "rocking and rolling." Because of the limits to what radio stations would play, slang terms such as these would often be used. The masses never knew what they meant. But, no one could dispute that Alan Freed, his fanatic audience, and their rousing rock and roll were undeniable realities.

Nonetheless, among white adults, R&B was considered to be low class black music. The conventional wisdom of the time was along the lines of, " . . . after all, if it is so much fun, and the lyrics are so raw and earthy, it certainly has to be trash." And since it was black-based, racists had a ball putting the music down, referring to it by such terms as "n——music" and "jungle music."

And with the advent of R&B music, music traditionalists were repulsed by this unsophisticated music form. To them, music should only have been performed and recorded by trained students of music. Imagine how offended they must have been by this upstart music, performed largely by less educated blacks and aimed at black audiences!

Radio also contributed to the lack of acceptance of early R&B. At the time radio was pretty much in harmony with traditional music and had no reason to be any less segregationist than any other industry. Therefore, the music played over the airwaves was pretty much what the like-minded record industry approved and promoted. So, the outlet for R&B music was severely limited. As a young listener, I sensed that this was the case, but didn't know it for sure until later. Considering such staunch opposition, it is nothing short of amazing that this music and its offshoots came to define an entire social force in America.

There was something else exciting happening in mainstream music at the same time. It was called "hillbilly music." Younger whites were beginning to perform hillbilly music and gradually incorporating the big beat influences of R&B. This music was centered in Nashville, Tennessee, mainly because of a program broadcast from the 50,000 watt, clear channel radio station WSM-AM. The program was "The Grand Ole Opry," and it could be heard throughout two thirds of the U.S. Aubrey and I spent many Saturday nights with Nana and Granddaddy listening to Minnie Pearl, Little Jimmy Dickens and Roy Acuff on their small radio and enjoying the corniness of it all.

This hillbilly music was viewed by society as lower class white music, and as "trashy" as R&B. And much to the dismay of parents, these two music forms were to combine certain characteristics, and become rock and roll.

CHAPTER 3

FROM RADIO TO THE JUKE BOX

My first-hand knowledge of music by the early 50's was limited. I had all that school imparted in flute and voice lessons and Mother insisted that I take piano lessons. Not only was the tedious repetition more than I could bear; far worse was that I didn't enjoy most of the music I was forced to play. But I knew what I did like, and what a lot of other kids liked, and that was R&B music. Thank goodness for the radio—and records I could play on my turntable. Since television was just budding, it beamed only to major markets. And even though all the neighbors came to look when Daddy and Betty got their first TV set, a bulky Zenith console, very few families owned television sets and radio was still dominant.

Local radio stations used "block programming" which combined local and network programs into slots or blocks. A typical day's line-up usually included the local morning personality playing records (in Greenville it was Bob Poole), followed by network programs like "Don McNeil's Breakfast Club" and "The Arthur Godfrey Show," and the local news, obituaries and farm reports at noon. The early afternoon slot featured network soap operas and game shows. After-school programs were typically aimed at children, and featured both local and network shows. My favorite was "The Lone Ranger. "The combined local and network news, sports, and weather began around 6 P.M.

The evening line-up was usually network programs. Millions of listeners, including Aubrey and I, tuned in religiously to such shows as "Amos 'n' Andy," "The Great Gildersleeve," "Edgar Bergen and Charlie McCarthy," "Bob Hope," "Burns and Allen," "Inner Sanctum," "The Shadow," "Jack Benny," "Dragnet," "Crimebusters," and "Fibber McGee and Molly." Most stations then signed off from midnight until early

12

morning.

As the decade progressed, hillbilly music, swap and shop formats, jazz or big band music, gospel and spiritual music, and R&B became popular during the late afternoon and evening. Both Aubrey and I knew the schedules of the Greenville stations by heart so we wouldn't miss our favorite shows after school.

My broadening education came from music programs aired on two Greenville stations. The first was called "Jam and Jive from Four to Five" and was heard on WMRC-AM. Hosted by disc jockey Jim Simpson, it featured pure R&B. I became addicted to Jim's show, because I was by then addicted to this music. I couldn't wait until four o'clock each afternoon for his theme song—"The Elks Parade" by Bobby Sherwood and his Orchestra—which signaled the show's beginning. Luckily for me, and the growing number of young listeners, another great show sprung up on rival station WESC-AM each afternoon. Called "The Ebony Swing Club," it was hosted by disc jockey Wally Mullinax. Wally's theme song, a piece called "Chicken Shack Boogie" by Amos Milburn soon led to a name change for the show. "The Chicken Shack Club" became a huge hit among both young blacks and whites in the upstate of South Carolina.

Soon black disc jockeys began broadcasting over the airwaves on Greenville radio. The first two I recall were Wilfred Walker and Cornell Blakely [who is still on the air today]. The first nighttime R&B-rock and roll show in Greenville was the Max Mace show on WMRB-AM, each week-day evening. It was followed by Johnny Batson's show on WFBC-AM, broadcast live from the teen canteen in Cleveland Park every Friday night. Both shows were extremely popular with kids.

In other parts of the country, similar shows were gaining popularity. In addition to Alan Freed in Cleveland, R&B DJ's were becoming celebrities in their own right in various other cities, including: Al Benson in Chicago, Jack "The Rapper" Gibson (who today hosts an annual R&B convention in Atlanta—the largest of its kind in the U.S.) in Chicago, Atlanta, Louisville, Miami, Bill Cook in Newark, Rufus Thomas in Memphis, Vernon Winslow ("Dr. Daddy-O") in New Orleans, and Jocko Henderson in Baltimore, Philadelphia, New York. Music fans who think that rap is a recent phenomenon obviously didn't hear these disc jockeys and their contemporaries back in the early 50's who cleverly, rapidly, and rhythmically rhymed everything they said. To me, that was the "original

13

rap," and they were fantastic!

One radio station that had a great influence on kids in the Southeast was WLAC-AM a 50,000 watt clear channel station that broadcast out of Nashville. From nightfall to daybreak the station beamed R&B to mostly black audiences. As with the radio shows in Greenville, we kids eagerly tuned in to the voices of the station's pied pipers: Gene Nobles, Bill "Hoss Man" Allen, Herman Grizzard, Hugh "Baby" Jarrett and John Richbourg (known as John R.). I didn't know it at the time, but John R. would later touch my life in a very special way.

The radio industry on the whole was very resistant to R&B and rock and roll music in its early days. It was a decade later before the industry gave in to the homogenized rock and roll wave; and R&B was never accepted as mainstream. Radio was as racist as any other segment of society, and was in close harmony with the Broadway, Hollywood, "good music"/major label dominated recording industry.

Music was becoming a big part of my life even then, but like most boys my age, I loved football, baseball, basketball, "Cowboys and Indians," playing "Army," roller skating and riding my bike. But whenever I could, I listened to music on the radio and increasingly, my friends were tuning in along with me and talking about our favorite records when we weren't listening to the music. For the most part our parents didn't really approve, but tolerated it, and considered the music to be just a passing fad. It was only in later years, after it was called rock and roll, that parental pressure really came into play. A possible exception might have been the time my mother purposely broke my 78 rpm copy of "Honey Love" by the Drifters over her knee exclaiming she wouldn't permit me to listen to such suggestive lyrics! Until her dramatics, I had never even paid attention to the words. After carefully listening to every word, I still couldn't understand her objections because it didn't seem "suggestive" to me—and, after all, I bought the records because they sounded good, not because of the lyrics. The record my mother broke, "Honey Love," was on the bright red and black Atlantic label.

Atlantic Records had been founded by a Turkish immigrant named Ahmet Ertegun in the late 40's. Headquartered in New York City, the label's roster included a virtual "who's who of R&B" throughout the decade of the 50's. A large percentage of my bulging record collection consisted of Atlantic records.

14

One of the first artists signed by Atlantic was an unforgettable singer named Ruth Brown. She was truly a classy, talented and versatile singer who had a way of wrapping her own style around a song. One of the first songs to take young listeners by storm was Ruth's "Mama, He Treats Your Daughter Mean." It was the first R&B record that all the kids at school went crazy over. Other big hits by Ruth include "Smooth Operator," "Five, Ten, Fifteen Hours," "Teardrops From Your Eyes," "Jack O'Diamonds," "This Little Girl's Gone Rockin'" and "Lucky Lips." Other early Atlantic artists were the Clovers, Joe Turner, Chuck Willis, Ray Charles, Lavern Baker, the Drifters, Clyde McPhatter and Ivory Joe Hunter.

The early 50's marked the beginning of the strong influence of the smaller, independent record labels (called "indies.") These labels turned out some of the freshest and best, most fun-filled music in history. The indies filled a gap, recording only what they felt the market demanded. They kept a sure finger on the pulse of the primary record-buyers—black and white teens, while the major labels were conservative and steadfastly refused to record R&B music, considering it to be only a fad. There was also a publishing war between ASCAP (American Society of Composers, Authors, and Publishers) and BMI (Broadcast Music Incorporated). The major labels were aligned with long established ASCAP and the indies with upstart BMI, which only furthered the resistance to R&B by radio and the "legitimate" recording industry. Although racism was a factor, more importantly, both radio and the major label establishment feared an erosion of their power base, thus their huge slice of the economic pie.

Major record labels at the time and their headliners included the following mainstream artists:

RCA Victor—Perry Como, Eddie Fisher, the Ames Brothers, Jaye P. Morgan and Kay Starr

Capitol—Frank Sinatra, Nat King Cole, Dean Martin, Tennessee Ernie Ford and Peggy Lee

Columbia—Doris Day, Rosemary Clooney, Johnny Mathis, the Four Lads, Johnnie Ray, Mitch Miller, Tony Bennett and Frankie Laine

Decca/Coral—Bing Crosby, Teresa Brewer, the Four Aces, the McGuire Sisters, Al Hibbler and Sammy Davis, Jr.

Mercury—Patti Page, Georgia Gibbs, the Crew Cuts, Dinah Washington and Sarah Vaughan

The major labels' roster was not very appealing to the average teenager, black or white. The indies saw an opportunity and dove in. For them it was mostly a money-making endeavor and not much altruism was shown to the artists who provided the vehicles for their success. Some of the independent label owners included the following: Syd Nathan of King, Federal and Deluxe; Lew Chudd of Imperial; Herman Lubinsky of Savoy; George Goldner of End and Gone; Hy Weiss of Old Town; Morris Levy of Roulette; Sam Phillips of Sun; Leonard Chess of Chess; Don Robey of Peacock; Jules, Joe, and Saul Bihari of Modern; Ed and Leo Mesner of Aladdin; James and Vivian Bracken, Calvin Carter of Vee-Jay and Art Rupe of Specialty.

Fredric Dannen in his book **Hit Men**[1] talks about independent label owners, " . . . Many of them were crooks. Their victims were usually poor blacks, the inventors of rock and roll, though whites did not fare much better. It was a common trick to pay off a black artist with a Cadillac worth a fraction of what he was owed. Special mention is due Herman Lubinsky, owner of Savoy Records in Newark, who recorded a star line-up of jazz, gospel, and rhythm and blues artists and paid scarcely a dime in royalties."

Nelson George in **The Death Of Rhythm & Blues**[2] explains, " . . Most indies were started by whites, many of them Jewish; blacks weren't the only people kept out of the American business mainstream by discrimination. Unwelcome on Wall Street, many Jewish businessmen looked for places where there were fewer barriers to entrepreneurship. They often turned to black neighborhoods—in some ways paralleling blacks' discovery that their avenues for advancement were less barricaded in the world of entertainment . . ."

In truth, most artists simply wanted the chance to record their music and perform for their fans; some had designs on getting rich, but most didn't give monetary gain that much thought. And record owners usually knew how to use the artists' naiveté and lack of business savvy to their own personal advantage.

Many artists have told me stories of how they were talked, even coerced, into selling the rights to songs they had written for $50 or $100—for the privilege and honor of becoming a recording artist. And in many cases, those songs have gone on to generate sales in the millions of dollars. Before his death, Jimmy Reed spoke candidly, "Well, there was some money made, but I didn't get it." My friends and I, as well as other teenagers throughout the U.S. bought millions of these records for about ninety cents each, unaware at the time that our favorite artists were being ripped off.

But without the indies, neither the music nor the artists would have had the chance to go even as far as they did. Granted, payola (the practice of paying radio DJ's to play records) reared its ugly head in getting air time for many records, but the success of these labels was mainly because they recorded what the market demanded. With just a modicum of exposure, sales of indie labels skyrocketed. These labels were responsible for such songs and artists from the 50's that became part of my permanent collection:

"Sixty Minute Man"-The Dominoes
"Money Honey"-The Drifters
"Honey Love"-The Drifters
"White Christmas"-The Drifters
"Fool, Fool, Fool"-The Clovers
"One Mint Julep"-The Clovers
"Devil Or Angel"-The Clovers
"Blue Velvet"-The Clovers
"Work With Me Annie"-The Midnighters
"Annie Had A Baby"-The Midnighters
"Sincerely"-The Moonglows
"Earth Angel"-The Penguins
"Wallflower"-Etta James
"Mary Lou"-Young Jessie
"Shake Rattle and Roll"-Joe Turner
"Flip Flop and Fly"-Joe Turner
"Tweedlee Dee"-Lavern Baker
"Pledging My Love"-Johnny Ace
"Ain't That A Shame"-Fats Domino
"Lawdy Miss Clawdy"-Lloyd Price
"I Hear You Knocking"-Smiley Lewis
"Hearts of Stone"-The Charms
"Close Your Eyes"-The 5 Keys
"Think"-The 5 Royales
"I Almost Lost My Mind"-Ivory Joe Hunter
"Mama He Treats Your Daughter Mean"-Ruth Brown
"Bo Diddley"-Bo Diddley
"Maybelline"-Chuck Berry

"Halleleujah I Love Her So"-Ray Charles
"Smokey Joe's Cafe"-The Coasters
"I'll Be Home"-The Flamingos
"Don't Be Angry"-Nappy Brown
"Crying In The Chapel"-The Orioles
"Sh-Boom"-The Chords

Sales of records by black artists increased "crossover" appeal to white kids. And seeing the popularity of the music among us teenagers, record companies (even major labels) realized there was a simple way to appeal to more kids. Using popular mainstream artists, they re-recorded songs that were already moving up the record charts. Radio stations that never would have aired the original black or country versions quickly played the homogenized versions.

This was the birth of the infamous "cover" record. The covers were tamer than the originals, and parents' fears were eased sufficiently to allow their kids to buy more records. Sales increased substantially—no thanks to my friends and me who thought the covers were pale comparisons, and at best, amusing. Examples of cover records and original artists covered are:

Song	Cover Version	Original Version
"Ain't That A Shame"	Pat Boone	Fats Domino
"Tutti Frutti"	Pat Boone	Little Richard
"Long Tall Sally"	Pat Boone	Little Richard
"I'll Be Home"	Pat Boone	The Flamingos
"Two Hearts, Two Kisses"	Pat Boone	The Charms
"Sincerely"	The McGuire Sisters	The Moonglows
"Earth Angel"	The Crew Cuts	The Penguins
"Sh-Boom"	The Crew Cuts	The Chords
"I Hear You Knocking"	Gale Storm	Smiley Lewis
"Only You"	The Hilltoppers	The Platters
"Hearts Of Stone"	The Fontane Sisters	The Charms
"Roll With Me Henry"	Georgia Gibbs	Etta James
"Tweedlee Dee"	Georgia Gibbs	Lavern Baker
"Ko Ko Mo"	Perry Como/The Crew Cuts	The Flamingos
"Little Darling"	The Diamonds	The Gladiolas
"Bo Weevil"	Teresa Brewer	Fats Domino
"Eddie My Love"	The Chordettes/The Fontane Sisters	The Teen Queens

"Rollin' Stone"	The Fontane Sisters	The Marigolds
"Pledging My Love"	Teresa Brewer	Johnny Ace
"You Send Me"	Teresa Brewer	Sam Cooke
"Shake Rattle & Roll"	Bill Haley	Joe Turner
"Blue Suede Shoes"	Elvis Presley	Carl Perkins
"Goodnight My Love"	The McGuire Sisters	Jesse Belvin
"Gum Drop"	The Crew Cuts	The Charms
"I'm Walkin'"	Ricky Nelson	Fats Domino
"Ka-Ding-Dong"	The Diamonds/	The G-Clefs
	The Hilltoppers	
"Love, Love, Love"	The Diamonds	The Clovers
"Rip It Up"	Bill Haley	Little Richard
"Later Alligator"	Bill Haley	Bobby Charles
"Silhouettes"	The Diamonds	The Rays
"Young Love"	Tab Hunter/The Crew Cuts	Sonny James

This sly trick of the record industry helped create the concept of the teenage idol. It was a good news-bad news scenario for the original black R&B and country artists as far as record sales were concerned. On one hand, the cover artist usually outsold the original artist; however the exposure given the song itself helped sell more copies of the original artist's record. [Time has proven the worth of the original versions as they have continued to sell throughout the years, while most cover versions quit selling in the 50's.]

David P. Szatmary in his book <u>Rockin' In Time</u>[3] explains, "The major record and publishing companies, songwriters, and disc jockeys refused to allow independent labels and their black artists to enjoy the success that they deserved. As Mick Jagger of the Rolling Stones once observed: 'Music is one of the things that changes society. The old idea of not letting white children listen to black music is true, 'cause if you want white children to remain what they are, they mustn't.'"

With all this going against it, how did R&B get even as far as it did? The juke box certainly played a part. Millions of kids were greatly influenced by what they heard on juke boxes in establishments throughout the country. Places that featured juke boxes often had areas for dancing, so it was natural that juke box operators provide as much danceable music as possible. R&B was the most danceable music of all, and there was no juke box censorship.

In the Carolinas, thousands of kids like me danced to juke box music at beach hangouts. When we returned home, we called our local radio stations to request our favorites. Gradually, stations began giving in to the sheer force of requests. There were similar occurrences in other parts of the U.S., and the R&B-rock and roll movement was well on its way. Juke box play also was part of the compilation of a record's popularity and its listing on the various record charts. Its importance is often overlooked by music historians, but without the juke box, rock and roll may never have happened.

1 Fredric Dannen. *Hit Men* (New York, 1990). p. 31.
2 Nelson George. *The Death Of Rhythm & Blues* (New York, 1988). p. 28.
3 David Szatmary. *Rockin' In Time* (Englewood Cliffs, N.J., 1987). pp. 31-32.

CHAPTER 4

ELVIS AND ROCKABILLY

My experience with the Elvis Presley phenomenon was something else again. When Elvis first arrived on the scene, I was in the ninth grade at Greenville Junior High School. At school kids basically fell into three groups. The fraternity and sorority kids were mostly children of affluent parents, while the middle group came from middle to middle-upper class parents. The lower income kids' parents mostly were textile mill workers. Since Greenville was known as "The Textile Center of the South", there were a lot of mill kids. These were the kids that rallied around Elvis. They wore slicked down hair, usually longer, and worn either in a pompadour style like Elvis, or swept back in a duck tail. Since Elvis came from a working class background, to these look-alike mill kids, he was an identifiable hero. The boys were attracted to his daring, defiant style, while the girls loved his sexy moves, good looks, and demeanor. But to the other kids in school Elvis was looked upon as "just another mill hick."

The term rockabilly (a contraction of rock and roll and hillbilly) came into vogue in 1956. Elvis had country and western roots via the Grand Ole Opry and many appearances on a country and western syndicated TV show called "Louisiana Hayride." So if there is an apt description of Elvis' specific style in his early years, it would be rockabilly.

Elvis was the single biggest reason for the infusion of rockabilly into mainstream rock and roll. Several Elvis sound-a-likes were to follow. One of the best of the lot was Conway Twitty. His 50's rock and roll hit called "It's Only Make Believe" is now considered a standard. Also, Bobby Bare, under the name of Bill Parsons, scored with a hit that parodied Elvis' career to that point. It was called "The All American Boy."

As rockabilly music began to make its presence known, there was one new song that I really liked, "Blue Suede Shoes" by Carl Perkins. A friend asked if I had heard "Blue Suede Shoes" by this hot new artist. I answered yes, adding, that I did not realize that Carl Perkins was a "hot" property. He said, "No, not Carl . . .some guy with a funny name . . . Elvis something." Almost immediately he was joined by more kids, also talking about Elvis Presley's version. Intriguingly, it wasn't that these kids preferred his version of the song, or were Elvis fans; they were simply curious about the commotion he was causing.

I made a bee-line to Mary's Record Shop to give it a listen. Those were the days when record shops had booths where customers could listen to records. Upon hearing Presley's version, my reaction was, "What's all the fuss about anyway?" I didn't think it was nearly as good as the original by Carl Perkins, which I promptly bought for my collection.

A couple of weeks later I was watching a variety show hosted by bandleaders Tommy and Jimmy Dorsey. There was a definite air of excitement as "the hillbilly cat," Elvis made his appearance, and I'm all but sure that there were some screams from some of the females in the audience. I was curious and thought it all kind of silly. He was okay as a performer, but as my preference was R&B, he was not my thing. I saw him as a flashy country and western singer attempting to sing R&B.

In short order, the excitement surrounding Elvis began to take on the trappings of hysteria among teenage girls everywhere. There still weren't many Presley fans, though, among my friends at school. Most of us guys preferred R&B artists, and Elvis' entrance onto the rock and roll scene did nothing to change our minds. However, after appearances on the nationally televised Ed Sullivan and Steve Allen shows, his popularity began to soar, and the mill kids adopted him as their hero.

It took a while longer before some of my friends became fans of his, but the sheer amount of publicity about Elvis began to make a difference with kids at school. Most of these kids were rebellious types with whom I didn't associate anyway, so I did not give it that much thought. There was the same admiration for his rebellious persona as there was for actors such as Marlon Brando and James Dean.

Then Richard Brassell and his family moved into the apartment building where we lived. Two things stood out about Richard. He was a strapping football lineman, and he was a real, true-blue Elvis Presley fan.

22

In fact, he had dark hair, which he wore slicked back in a pompadour style similar to Elvis. And the Elvis look worked very well for Richard. Guys were jealous because he dated gorgeous Ginger, the girl who filled out her sweaters better than any other girl at school. Even though he was my only good friend who was an Elvis fan, it made me realize that Elvis' influence was spreading further than just silly, giggling girls and the mill kids at school.

Despite the slow acceptance of Elvis by my friends and me, it was now apparent that he was the biggest star on the music scene. With the beginning of his movie career, marked by the release of **Love Me Tender**, co-starring Richard Egan and Debra Paget, he became just about the biggest star in the entertainment industry, period.

Elvis' only failure after he became popular was an ill-timed 50's Las Vegas appearance. His manager, Colonel Tom Parker always had an affinity for Las Vegas, but this time his judgment was off-target. The strip's entertainment was totally dominated by mainstream pop music artists and was simply not ready for Elvis. While he was in Vegas, Elvis repeatedly caught a lounge act that bowled him over—the Dominoes. He describes watching them perform his hit "Don't Be Cruel" in <u>Good Rockin' Tonight</u> by Colin Escott: "'I heard this guy in Las Vegas—Billy Ward and his Dominoes. There's a guy out there who's doin' a take-off on me—'Don't Be Cruel.' He tried so hard, till he got much better, boy-much better than that record of mine.

. . . He had it a little slower than me . . . He got the backin', the whole quartet. They got the feelin' on in . . . Grabbed that microphone, went down to the last note, went all the way down to the floor, man, lookin' straight up at the ceiling. Man, he cut me—I was under the table when he got through singin' . . .

. . . I went back four nights straight and heard that guy do that. Man, he sung hell outta that song, and I was under the table lookin' at him. Git him off! Git him off!'

Escott adds, "Although Presley probably didn't know it, the singer he was watching must have been Jackie Wilson, then the lead singer with Billy Ward's Dominoes." It reveals just how much even Presley appreciated authentic R&B.

His first number one record was "Heartbreak Hotel" in 1956. It was followed by a string of number one hits in succession, including, "I

Want You, I Need You, I Love You," "Teddy Bear," "Don't Be Cruel" backed by "Hound Dog," "All Shook Up," and the title song from his first movie, "Love Me Tender." I liked most of them but bought only a few as my money was spent to buy records by Fats Domino, Joe Turner, Ray Charles, the Drifters, Clyde McPhatter, Ruth Brown, Chuck Berry, the Coasters, Lavern Baker, Little Richard, Bo Diddley, and even rockabilly favorites like Jerry Lee Lewis, Buddy Knox, Gene Vincent and Carl Perkins.

I was genuinely fond of the upbeat, good-time feel and sound of white-based, country-flavored rockabilly. But I felt that it was taking the play from the original black R&B based rock and roll, which I loved best—and, since there was no place at that time in country and western music for blacks, I wondered, why there was a place in black-based rock and roll music for country and western singers? Black country and western singer Charley Pride didn't break that barrier until more than a decade later. It has been said that if more country music industry movers and shakers had known Pride was black before his records began to hit the charts that it wouldn't have happened.

Paul Hemphill explains in his book, The Nashville Sound: Bright Lights and Country Music, " . . . This was country music as recently as 1960, when the rock 'n' roll craze had so taken hold that there were no more than eighty radio stations in the United States that carried country music on a full-time basis; and those stations, generally speaking, were having to hack it out in the deep backwoods with an offering of jakeleg radio preachers and corny disc jockeys who frantically tried to hold their listeners by convincing them that rock 'n' roll was inherently sinful and was, after all, nothing more than 'nigger music."' Though many fans accepted rockabilly, their prejudicial thinking precluded their approval of rock and roll, with its black R&B foundation. It took me a while, because of this hypocrisy, to accept rockabilly and understand how and why it came to be in the first place. Today, I have a real love for this special segment of rock and roll, and feel that its contributions are much underappreciated.

By the mid-50's hillbilly music had undergone a name change and was being called country and western. A few of its artists had begun branching out into the popular and rock and roll fields through the rest of the decade. Some examples were:

Marty Robbins (Columbia)-"A White Sport Coat"
Sonny James (Capitol)-"Young Love"
Ferlin Husky (Capitol)-"Gone"
Patsy Cline (Decca)-"Walkin' After Midnight"
Webb Pierce (Decca)-"I Ain't Never"
Don Gibson (RCA Victor)-"Oh Lonesome Me"
Jim Reeves (RCA Victor)-"Four Walls"

Their records, all on major labels, had as many pop music over-tones as country, and some rock and roll influence was obvious. For eco-nomic reasons, the majors were encouraging country music to broaden its base of appeal.

Country and western was separated from rock and roll by the noticeable lack of drums and from pop by the extreme nasal twang of the singers' voices. The driving snare drum back beat—the big beat—was one of the main cogs in the wheel of rock and roll, so, the producers added drums to entice rock and roll fans. They also minimized the nasal twang on songs and even added choruses to reach fans of mainstream popular.

We rock and roll fans didn't know the difference between major label attempts to reach us with well-known country singers, and pure rockabilly which was mainly recorded on the independent labels by unknown singers. To us it was all rockabilly. We didn't mind the nasal twang as long as the driving beat was present. One of the all time rocka-billy classics is "Party Doll" by Buddy Knox on the independent Roulette label. Throughout the record, Buddy pronounced the word hair as "har" and, he had a slight nasal twang to his voice; but, unmistakably, the driv-ing beat played prominently in the background.

Other than the cover artists of the old school, the majority of the white stars of early rock and roll were of the rockabilly type. Oddly, in those days, female singers of pure rock and roll were practically non-exis-tent. The first, and almost only, female rock and roll stars of the day were black Atlantic recording artists, Lavern Baker and Ruth Brown. The first white female star of rock and roll was Connie Francis; shortly thereafter, the first female rockabilly rock and roll star arrived on the scene. She was referred to as "Little Miss Dynamite," and I remember hearing the rumor that she was a grown up midget with a young sounding voice. Her name was Brenda Lee.

Some examples of rockabilly artists and their hit records are:

The Everly Brothers-"Bye Bye Love," "Wake Up Little Suzie," "Bird Dog"
Gene Vincent-"Be Bop A Lula," "Lotta Lovin"'
Eddie Cochran-"Somethin' Else," "Summertime Blues," "Twenty Flight Rock"
Joe Bennett and the Sparkletones-"Black Slacks"
Carl Perkins-"Blue Suede Shoes," "Honey Don't"
Jerry Lee Lewis-"Whole Lot Of Shakin' Going On," "Great Balls of Fire,"
    "Breathless"
Charlie Rich-"Lonely Weekends"
Buddy Knox-"Party Doll," "Hula Love," "Rock Your Little Baby To Sleep"
Jimmy Bowen-"I'm Stickin' With You"
Ray Smith-"Rockin' Little Angel"
Johnny Burnette-"Dreamin'," "You're Sixteen"
Buddy Holly and the Crickets-"That'll Be The Day," "Oh Boy," Peggy Sue," "Maybe
    Baby"
Carl Mann-"Mona Lisa"
Bob Luman-"Let's Think About Living"
Ricky Nelson-"Believe What You Say," "Stood Up," "It's Late," "Hello Mary Lou,"
    "Travelin' Man"
Roy Orbison-"Uptown," "Only The Lonely"
Brenda Lee-"That's All You Gotta Do," "Sweet Nothin's"
Ray Sharpe-"Linda Lu"
Wanda Jackson-"Let's Have A Party"
Dorsey Burnette-"A Tall Oak Tree"

The heyday of rockabilly was during the late 50's. Its momentum was damaged by Elvis Presley's induction into the service and the more sophisticated and "cuter" teen idols. Had Elvis continued in his rockabilly tradition after his discharge, rockabilly would have probably remained strong. But Colonel Parker had his eyes focused on Hollywood, and the rockabilly Elvis would soon become a thing of the past.

4 Colin Escott, *Good Rockin' Tonight* (New York, 1991). pp. 88-89.
5 Paul Hemphill, *The Nashville Sound: Bright Lights and Country Music* (New York, 1970). pp. 175-176.

CHAPTER 5

TEENAGE YEARS

While rock and roll was changing, Aubrey and I spent weekends and summers in Ware Shoals and attended school in Greenville. During that time I also met Junior, who became one of my closest friends. He was the son of Gyland, my father's handy man. Junior and I would spend our time together playing sports and talking about and listening to R&B music. It never seemed often enough that we saw each other. We had so much in common and we never argued. We confided in each other our deepest secrets, and shared a deep, mutual understanding.

Yet, Junior and I always played as a twosome and didn't join the rest of my friends though the other kids would have welcomed it. It was not discouraged, it just seemed to have been presumed. Even so, we were living proof that a black boy and a white boy could be close friends in the South in the 50's, despite the pressures of the time against such a possibility.

For the most part, Aubrey and I occupied the long, hot, summer days swimming at the community pool, going to movies, and playing the local nine hole golf course. I must have seen my favorite movie **The Greatest Show On Earth** with Charlton Heston, Betty Hutton and James Stewart at least ten times. And, though I played golf almost every day, to break ninety was a God-send.

We guys were also discovering girls. Toddy Mauldin often spent the night. My bedroom had an intercom, so my folks could listen in. Forgetting that the intercom was there, Toddy, one year older and wiser, began to authoritatively dispense information about the sexual desires of the opposite sex. That was followed by numerous dirty jokes and snickering until the wee hours of the morning. What an earful Daddy and Betty must have gotten.

We kids usually had to entertain ourselves, so we devised our own games, compared to highly organized sports for kids today. We transformed grassy lots into measured football fields and sculptured baseball diamonds. Sometimes we had as many as a whole neighborhood of twenty or more. Serving as our own officials, we all took the rules quite seriously. Anyone caught cheating was promptly tossed from the game; interestingly, that rarely happened. I don't remember our parents ever coming to watch us play. Parents today seem to dog their kids' every move. I'm glad ours didn't, as I would not have welcomed the scrutiny and pressure to perform to adult standards.

On rainy days we had to be especially creative. J.J. Valter and I concocted games that we played inside by using football and baseball bubble gum trading cards. We invented our own rules by flipping the cards and applying certain values to the star status of each player's cards. These games were so much fun that quite often, even when the weather cleared, we could be found inside still flipping away.

With our penchant for inventing games, it was only natural for us to come up with a music game. J.J., Ralph Hardeman, Aubrey and I designed our own weekly "Hit Parade" charts. "Your Hit Parade" was the popular weekly radio and television program which featured a regular cast of singers who performed the seven top hits on that week's chart. The regular singers were Dorothy Collins, Gisele MacKenzie, Snooky Lanson and Russell Arms. Each of us spent time each week going up and down the radio dial, and recording every song we heard. We then tallied our marks, combined them, and published our own "Hit Parade." We eagerly anticipated each week's compilation and found the results most interesting—closely resembling what the regional and national charts would show a week or two later. Some monster songs on our charts were "Searchin'" by the Coasters, "Twilight Time" by the Platters, "Rock Around The Clock" by Bill Haley and the Comets, "Hearts Of Stone" by the Charms, "Sweet Little Sixteen" by Chuck Berry, "Jim Dandy" by Lavern Baker, "Heartbreak Hotel" by Elvis Presley, "I'm In Love Again" by Fats Domino, "Tutti Frutti" by Little Richard, "Love Letters In The Sand" by Pat Boone, "What Am I Living For" by Chuck Willis, "Party Doll" by Buddy Knox, and "Wake Up Little Suzie" by the Everly Brothers.

Our parents often had parties for us at the Ware Shoals Golf Course clubhouse where we could dance to juke box music. Most of the music was mainstream popular, but I do clearly remember trying to shag to "One Mint Julep" by the Clovers. Ralph, J.J. and I spent hours working up a couple of lip-synching routines which we "performed" at one party to two good-time records—"Rock And Roll Is Here To Stay" by Danny and the Juniors, and "Don't You Just Know It" by Huey Smith and the Clowns. We had a ball hamming it up.

It's silly as I think about it now, but I remember being ashamed to tell sophisticated "big-city" Greenville schoolmates that I was going to the mill town of Ware Shoals on week-ends. I guess I was afraid that I would be looked down upon as lower class. Whether I wanted to admit it or not, I was not immune to a certain amount of peer pressure.

Many of my classmates were beginning to be motivated more by the "in" group than by what they really liked. Cruising was a hoot to most of the guys, but not me. I couldn't understand the thrill it gave them to drive around the Clock drive-in every weekend night time and time again, with horns and radios blaring, to see the same people they had just been with a few hours earlier. As a very reluctant cruiser, I took my mother's green 1949 Chevrolet sedan when I went out at night. It's funny to talk to old school chums today and hear many of them admit that they, too, felt cruising was a waste of time and gas.

The fraternity and sorority kids sponsored dances held at the Poinsett Hotel with live big bands like Tommy Dorsey and Glenn Miller. Reluctantly, I attended a few of them, but the dances bored me to tears. Nevertheless I found myself, along with classmates Steve Young and Alex Zipperer, attending dance classes at the Greenville Hotel ballroom every Saturday night. For the life of me I couldn't understand why we had to learn the foxtrot, the waltz, the tango, and the rhumba. The music we danced to was played by a three piece combo and the loudest beat was nothing more than the faint brush on a cymbal. Give me some R&B with a driving backbeat and teach me to shag! Nonetheless, there we were, a mass of stiff Sunday suits and crinoline dresses, moving like a herd of brooms.

From time to time there were school-sponsored dances, which were chaperoned by both teachers and parents. The "sock hops," as they came to be called, were held in the gymnasium so shoes had to be left at the door and we danced in our socks. Most of the girls quickly gravitated as if by magnetic force to chairs placed against the wall and wouldn't budge. The boys were equally riveted to their chairs—but on the opposite side of the gym. There was almost no rock and roll allowed ("too corrupting")—mostly "popular" music. But we had shag contests to the pop music, and often kids had to be cajoled into getting on the dance floor. Richard Brassell won one of the contests, and was immediately accused by the second place dancer of doing the "dirty shag"—because of excessive wiggling.

Some of my friends in school were very much into music, like I was. Bobby Scales and Robert Waldrop both dabbled at playing guitar, and we talked about music constantly. Bobby's claim to fame was that he could expertly pick out the guitar solo of Bill Doggett's perfectly-titled hit, "Honky Tonk," and played it for us every chance he got. Robert became a super fan of Chuck Berry. In our high school annual, the Nautilus, is a note from Robert saying, "Let's keep Chuck on top!"

Each summer Daddy and Betty rented a beach cottage on the Grand Strand of South Carolina. Aubrey, my half-sisters Allison, Bootsie, Beth, Dottie and I eagerly packed our swim suits and shorts in anticipation of these fun-filled trips. Ocean Drive, Crescent Beach, Cherry Grove, Surfside Beach, Pawleys Island, Garden City, and fabled Myrtle Beach come to mind. We stayed at every one of those beaches, but Ocean Drive (known as "OD") was my favorite because that is where we stayed at the "polka dot house". It was a two story cottage covered with brilliant, multi-colored polka dots, and it could be "spotted" from both the road and the beach. Shrieks of laughter could be heard coming through the open windows, since there was no air-conditioning. We swam in the surf, rode the waves, played games on the beach, flew kites, fished and crabbed and played golf—and ate our fill of the abundant seafood at Murrell's Inlet.

Public beaches were segregated in the 50's and there was only one beach for blacks in South Carolina—Atlantic Beach. Several times each vacation we would take housekeepers Irene or Lillian to Atlantic Beach for an evening out. I always had to go along with my parents to drop her off so I could hear the "cutting edge" music that blared from the jiving beach hangouts nestled near the sand dunes. What was playing at

Atlantic Beach was what we kids would be dancing and listening to shortly thereafter.

One evening several of us drove Daddy's green and white 1956 Dodge station wagon to the Crescent Beach fishing pier for something to do. It was a beautiful, clear night and we could see the lights twinkling from Atlantic Beach in the distance. We were just within ear shot, and could catch the soulful R&B music drifting from the juke boxes. Forever woven into that evening is the melodic, up-tempo "Come What May" by Clyde McPhatter. It was the first time I had ever heard it, and it later became a moderate hit for Clyde. (Elvis would later record it.) We stayed on the pier for hours, listening, talking and dancing and secretly wishing we could be at Atlantic Beach.

As a teenager, the beach night life at the ocean-side pavilions became much more enticing. The smell of popcorn, cotton candy and french fries filled the humid night air. There was a blur of activity around the pavilions where R&B music blared from the juke boxes. It was a little piece of heaven for a young teenage boy and his shy teenage friends.

But even at the beach there were lessons to be learned. Toddy and I had spent the afternoon roaming the strip at "OD" and bought what we thought were really "cool" Mexican-style straw hats. The hats were about the size of small umbrellas, and even sported a nifty fringe. However, our ability to see out from underneath five pounds of straw was greatly limited. The cool, shagging crowd at the OD pavilion that night was somewhat older and definitely more sophisticated. And there we were two young boys with our "dynamite" hats, milling through the crowd, relishing the beautiful girls, feeling the ocean breeze, and listening to Fats Domino's "I'm In Love Again" blaring from the juke box.

Suddenly, our prized straw hats were snatched from our heads, and I looked around to see a well-tanned, muscular, lifeguard type stomping the hats with his Bass Weejuns as the crowd cheered lustily. With a wagging finger, he threateningly informed us, "Only idiots come to dance here with pieces of straw like that. When you two can get with the program, you're welcome." We were finding that even at the beach, there was an expected dress code and behavior.

The beach seemed to be the likely place for a first summertime fling. Her name was Judy and she, too, was vacationing with her parents. No question, I became quite smitten with Judy and liked to sing her the

Bobby Darin song "Judy, Don't Be Moody," the flip side of his smash hit "Splish Splash." But "our" special song was "One Summer Night" by the Danleers. We must have heard it ten times that last evening on the car radio as we parked in the moonlight and "made out," bathed in a mist of salt air. How I missed her when we had to go home and back to our routines, knowing that the magic we had shared was as fleeting as "One Summer Night." Sure enough, I saw her only one other time—it was not the same and, like most summer romances, we eventually lost touch. Still to this day, whenever I hear the sweet sounds of the Danleers singing that song, a wave of nostalgia rushes over me.

Despite the life my friends and I were living and loving, the media and the entertainment industry had other designs to fit their grandiose money-making plans to reach the newly found "baby-boom" population. Its effects were to be profound as life began to imitate art .

CHAPTER 6

ROCKIN' ON BANDSTAND

During the 50's there was a gradual change in the portrayal of the attitudes of teenagers and young adults in movies. In television's early days, they were still depicted as carefree types from loving, nurturing families. Who can forget the happy, lovable Nelson family with sons David and Ricky on "The Adventures of Ozzie and Harriett" or Jim Anderson, and wife Betty, with zany son Bud, and the wide-eyed, innocent daughters "Princess" and "Kitten," all of whom knew that "Father Knows Best?" These shows were syrupy but I liked even less what I was seeing on the big screen and was beginning to filter into other areas of entertainment including music.

Until the 50's, most unsavory movie characters were adults; very few were young people. The first young mischief makers I remember were those in the **Dead End Kids** and **The Bowery Boys** that starred Leo Gorcey and Huntz Hall. But they were harmless, likable klutzy teenagers.

The earliest change in attitude came with three Marlon Brando movies that featured Brando playing mixed-up, sneering, rebellious characters. The films were **The Wild One, On the Waterfront** and **A Streetcar Named Desire.** Today's cult hero James Dean, also played the misfit and bad boy image—even Paul Newman had early roles that cast him in somewhat the same light with characters that were offensive and repulsive.

Then along came the seamy **Blackboard Jungle** starring Glenn Ford and Sidney Poitier which portrayed violent, rebellious punks in a New York City high school. The movie was a huge hit and had the all-time rock and roll classic, "Rock Around The Clock" by Bill Haley and the Comets as its theme song. The hoodlum teenagers were vicious and

33

unfeelingly cruel—far cries from the Bowery boys. Since I had already started my record collection at the time, the scene where the thugs took the teacher's treasured jazz records and smashed them to bits, sent cold shivers up my spine. I was also concerned that some of the trouble-making mill kids at my junior high wore their hair long and greasy and liked to fight—they were disturbingly similar to the ruffians in **Blackboard Jungle** who were becoming their role models.

In his book **Big Beat Heat**[6], John A. Jackson explains, "In the 1953 movie 'The Wild One,' based on a true story of a motorcycle gang that terrorized a small California town, a leather-clad biker played by Marlon Brando is asked what he is rebelling against. 'Whaddaya got? ' Brando replies. That scene pretty much summed up the attitude of a small yet highly visible portion of America's teenagers in the mid-1950's . . . This attitude was seized upon by the pop music business, which realized that rock & roll, which teenagers were adopting as their own music, could be marketed as a form of escapism and rebellion for them. The music business thus sought to exploit teenage tastes in order to broaden its own range of listeners."

Because of **Blackboard Jungle** and its theme song "Rock Around The Clock," rock and roll began to be associated with the thug teenage element. Jackson explains further, " . . providing 'proof' of the evils of rock & roll to another group of critics who feared and loathed it for a deeper and more passionate reason." The link between rock and roll and violence fueled the underlying reason many parents disliked rock and roll music; namely, racial prejudice and fears of interracial dating and marriage.

Teenage movie-goers, who were a part of the new post-war materialism, became jaded and were looking for something new to grab their attention. Nothing could have been more exciting to overindulged, immature teenagers than the idea of living on the edge as glamorized in movies such as **Rebel Without A Cause** starring James Dean, Natalie Wood, and Sal Mineo. Hollywood and the entertainment industry created, promoted, and even thrust this teenage image and attitude onto the American scene, and many teenagers, including some of my friends, bought it—hook, line and sinker.

Hollywood followed with several B-grade movies about rock and roll—with the rock and roll artists relegated to secondary, cameo appearances. These movies, however, as opposed to the Brando types, had very little story line, and continued to portray teenagers in a more fun-loving, innocent light. Hit rock and roll songs were interwoven with the "plots." Among the movies and artists who appeared in them were:

Rock, Rock, Rock-Lavern Baker, Chuck Berry, the Flamingos, the Moonglows and
       Frankie Lymon and the Teenagers
Shake, Rattle and Rock-Fats Domino and Joe Turner
Don't Knock The Rock-Bill Haley and the Comets and the Platters
Go Johnny Go-Jimmy Clanton and Chuck Berry
Teenage Millionaire-Jimmy Clanton and Marv Johnson
The Girl Can't Help It-Fats Domino, Little Richard, the Platters, Gene Vincent and
      Eddie Cochran

Nonetheless, the bored, rebellious attitude portrayed in movies aimed at young people began to seep into musical tastes. The pouting Elvis adopted the image and bore this mantle until the mid-60's when, with the British music invasion, rebellion soared to even greater heights.

Throughout most of the 50's there were pronounced regional differences in rock and roll. DJ's were the hit makers, and had enormous regional influence; plus they had freedom and control over what records they played. They became celebrities in their own rights and independent record labels courted these "pied pipers of the airwaves" with payola. Radio began employing the extremely popular "Top 40" music format and DJ's were its beneficiaries and radio's reigning royalty.

Though Hollywood movies had given rock and roll wide exposure, there was no national TV or radio show devoted to rock and roll. In 1957, rock and roll was in full swing, with an energy unparalleled in the history of recorded music. Timing could not have been better for a national rock and roll dance program. Originally hosted by Bob Horn, a live teenage dance show had been broadcasting since 1952 on WFIL-TV in Philadelphia, Pennsylvania. Its host since July 1956, was a boyish, clean-cut gentleman named Dick Clark who boasted a gleaming smile. The show was a smashing success. ABC-TV was the maverick network of the "big three" and was looking for new and unique programming. As number three in networks ratings, they were willing to take a chance. And so, on Monday, August 5, 1957, at 3 P.M., that show, American Bandstand, became a national show when ABC began telecasting each afternoon Monday through Friday on sixty-seven stations coast to coast. It changed the after school routines of many school kids, including Aubrey and me.

Whether a master stroke of programming genius, pure luck, or a combination of both, the country truly was ready for a show of its type. The main reason for its success, other than the music, was its "all-American" host, Dick Clark. How could parents take offense at rock and roll if that "nice Dick Clark" was the one playing it over the television airwaves and into their living rooms? It even made Chuck Berry more palatable to my parents.

Before American Bandstand there were only two major teen idols. One was Elvis; the other was Pat Boone. Boone was really not a rock and roll artist, but because he covered rock and roll songs by other artists, some considered him a rock and roll singer. Pat has been given a bum rap ever since because of his inferior cover records. In reality he did an excellent job on his original hits such as, "Love Letters In The Sand" and "April Love."

With American Bandstand, teenagers had a forum of their own for the first time. They had input as to what they wanted in the way of music, dance, features, and even the artists who would appear on the show. But it was one thing for a teenager to hear a song on the radio and something else again to see the artist perform on television. After the advent of American Bandstand, teenagers became more influenced by an artist's appearance than how the artist sounded. This was the real birth of the infamous teenage idol. Some teen idols were talented, like Paul Anka and Bobby Rydell, but most were "groomed" by the industry because they were good-looking, but had questionable talent. Their flaws were well covered up by talented recording studio engineers. It didn't matter when they appeared on American Bandstand anyway because they lip-synched their hits. This was the beginning of the decline in substance and fun in the music and the beginning of the importance of sex appeal, gimmickry, and hype.

The most well-known teen idol was Fabian Forte. He was a strikingly handsome boy who was reputedly discovered on the streets of Philadelphia. His movie star good looks was reason enough to manufacture him into a rock and roll star. And did it ever work! Wildly enthusiastic female audiences screamed feverishly during his live performances.

36

My friend Joe Bennett, lead singer of the rockabilly group, Joe Bennett and the Sparkletones, told me that he once backed Fabian in concert and that Fabian changed keys four times during one song, but nobody knew it except Joe and the other band members—because of the constant screaming, the girls surely didn't. As I watched Fabian on TV, I couldn't believe that American Bandstand could stoop so low. Other than the later hysteria over 60's British acts, that was as disgusted and frustrated as I have ever been as to the blatant promotion of an inferior product.

After a few months on the air, American Bandstand's popularity had made rock and roll a national music form. Regional differences, and the power of local DJ's began to wane. If a record was played on Bandstand, it all but guaranteed that it would become a hit. Credit should be given to Dick Clark and the show's producers because they did not refuse to play R&B music and I'm willing to bet that there were pressures brought to bear. Clark seemed to be genuinely fond of the music he played, and R&B appeared to be his favorite. Still . . .

As the show evolved, it became totally dedicated to the teenager. Dick Clark became somewhat of a big brother to teens as well as an enthusiastic TV host. It was not long before American Bandstand had garnered a huge, loyal teenage audience. Despite what a R&B purist like myself may have wanted, American Bandstand was on the air to make money for itself and ABC-TV. What better way than to offer the primarily female audience young, white, attractive, sexy male singers? With Dick Clark and his Bandstand cronies, "Mama didn't raise no fools!"

Not long after it went on the air, Bandstand became the home to almost every potential teen idol to be thrust onto the rock and roll scene. The show continued playing music by black R&B artists and featured them as guests. But the emphasis gradually shifted away from them for obvious reasons. The teen idols, like pretenders to the throne, were becoming a major force in rock and roll.

Despite Elvis' popularity, most of the other teen idols were not of the rebellious type. They were clean-cut looking and dressed mainly in suits or tuxedos. Other than the questionable singing talents of some of them, what parents objected to were the longer, greasy hair styles that they sported.

With black entertainers, polished dress was also a must. Male singers wore suits and female singers wore evening dresses. Nonetheless, since the 70's original rock and roll performers, both black and white, have been incorrectly portrayed as the **Blackboard Jungle** punk, rough-neck personified by Sha-Na-Na, the 50's parody singing group, and by Fonzie on the TV show "Happy Days." Entertainers from that era looked nothing at all like these Hollywood directors' inventions. Rudy West, the great tenor lead singer of the Five Keys once told me that Sha-Na-Na's dress and irreverent behavior were affronts to 50's groups and that, "We always dressed well for the people."

The time of the rock and roll teen idols' greatest vigor was from 1956 when Elvis gyrated onto the scene until 1964 with the advent of the Beatles. In the late 50's Elvis Presley was inducted into the army for a two-year stint overseas. If there were ever a time for a take over as the king of rock and roll, it would have been then. Elvis was the king; he had talent and a charisma that the teen idols plainly lacked. He was to reign unchallenged until early 1964, when four kings were crowned from across the ocean, and rock and roll went international.

The teen idols' popularity was never as strong in the southern states. Maybe it was because of general resistance on the part of Southerners or because many of the R&B and rockabilly stars were from that part of the country. Whatever the reasons, during the height of their popularity, a touring rock and roll show came to Columbia, S.C., that starred Fats Domino but featured a couple of teen idols as well. One of these hapless singers had the misfortune to come on before Fats, who was the headliner and final act for the evening. During his mediocre performance we in the crowd began stomping our feet and yelling loudly "We want Fats! We want Fats!" We received the disarming Fats with wild enthusiasm and a standing ovation, and his performance matched his reception. Much to our delight that evening, the clock was turned back briefly, as substance won out over hype.

6 John Jackson, *Big Beat Heat* (New York, 1991). pp. 123-124.

CHAPTER 7

THE GREAT ROCK AND ROLL SHOWS

It was during the middle 50's that the popular "packaged" rock and roll tours came through Greenville on a regular basis. The best of the shows was the annual "Biggest Show of Stars" presented by Super Attractions. These shows were produced by Irving and Kenneth Feld, who now own the Ringling Brothers and Barnum and Bailey Circus—**The Greatest Show on Earth.** That title certainly fit these shows, because they really were the greatest touring rock and roll shows ever presented and were some of the best entertainment values in history. In fact, they would have been a great value at any price.

The Feld shows consisted of about ten acts and each act had national hit records when they toured. To avoid delays between acts, there was a house orchestra, like Paul Williams and his big band, backing most of the singers. Those days rarely saw outdoor shows. The shows were usually held in large auditoriums, huge exhibition halls, or coliseums, and were first rate productions that fit the classy venues. The attention of the spectators was riveted on the performers, and spontaneous dancing often broke out in the aisles, which only added to the shows' electric atmosphere. There were only minimal detractions of spectators wandering around or talking during performances, whereas today, shows are often loosely run, and performers are rudely ignored by excessive moving around or loud conversation.

The acts were sharp, well-dressed, well-rehearsed, and sounded almost identical to the recordings they performed. In fact, the shows moved along at a rapid clip, as the artists took the stage, expertly performed their hits, and were quickly followed by the next act. A typical line-up consisted of artists like Fats Domino, Clyde McPhatter, Sam

Cooke, Lloyd Price, Chuck Berry, Bill Haley & the Comets, Bo Diddley, Little Anthony & the Imperials, Duane Eddy and Marv Johnson. I'm randomly listing names, but each of these acts did come to Greenville between 1955 and 1962. The shows would almost always sell out, and I have been told that Greenville was known as a good rock and roll town during those days. The cost of the shows ranged from $2 to $3 a seat. Aside from the price, imagine a regular tour featuring such a string of hit performers today! Over time, audiences have grown accustomed to a warm-up act and one name performer or group—for ten to fifteen times that price. What a difference three decades has made!

In the early days of rock and roll, the seating was segregated by race. It was the black audience which got the main floor, as these shows were expressly geared to black audiences and whites were relegated to the balcony. Soon afterwards, whites and blacks were seated on the main floor as well as the balcony, but in their own designated sections with the sections separated by ropes. In 1959, I remember leaning across the rope and glad-handing with a black friend named Smitty, who worked just down the street from the theater where I worked at the time. At many of the shows, there were blacks and whites acting like Smitty and me, in an equally happy, friendly manner. Left to its own devices, early rock and roll music brought divergent people together in a refreshingly innocent, natural, spontaneous and harmonious manner. John Jackson, in his **Big Beat Heat**[7], claims, " . . . The socially oriented attack on rock & roll originated in America's Southern regions where, by the time of 'The Blackboard Jungle's release, teenage-dance promoter Howard Lewis reported that rhythm and blues had become 'a potent force in breaking down racial barriers.'

" . . . Rhythm and blues producer Ralph Bass thought early rock & roll did as much to break down America's racial barriers as the civil rights acts and marches did. . . ." Those shows that I attended were the entertainment highlights of my life. After lo these thirty plus years, nothing else has come close.

Much like Ahmet Ertegun of Atlantic Records, I don't believe that Irving and Kenneth Feld had a true appreciation of just how good their shows were—much less a comprehension of the quality of the talent they amassed. They most probably viewed rock and roll as a vehicle for financial success and nothing more than a passing fad. It is my guess that they didn't give much thought to the phenomenal artistic merit of the emerging genre.

The black entertainers for these touring shows really must have loved pleasing an audience because of the humiliation and degradation that they encountered on the road at that time. And there we were, a be-boppin' bunch of white kids in ecstasy over their incredible performances, not realizing they were forced to scrounge to find a decent meal and a place to sleep. Actually, it was a matter of course that artists like Billie Holiday, Lena Horne, Count Basie, Lionel Hampton, Fats Domino, Chuck Berry and Bo Diddley stayed in private homes with black families when appearing in cities such as Greenville.

A personal scrapbook of memories of those dazzling shows has not dimmed:

* Jackie Wilson's voice, moves, dancing and doing the split, culminating in a graceful slide back into an upright position;
* The energy and fun antics of Chuck Berry highlighted, of course, by his patented "duck walk";
* Jimmy Jones, of "Handy Man" and "Good Timin'" fame, actually doing a backflip during his performance;
* Little Anthony and the Imperials and their individual dance routines;
* Lloyd Price, backed by his orchestra and chorus, singing "Stagger Lee," capped by a long chain of "oh yeah!" being shouted to and answered back by the audience;
* Sammy Turner's seductive tenor voice singing my favorite slow-dancing ballad of the summer of 1959, "Lavender Blue";
* Freddy "Boom Boom" Cannon's driving good-time style of rock and roll, doubling the validity of his nickname:
* Lead singer Johnny Maestro and the deeply pleasing harmonies of one of the first integrated singing groups, the Crests;
* The smooth style, immense talent and captivating charisma of Sam Cooke;
* Brook Benton doing masterful impersonations of Fats Domino and Roy Hamilton;
* The show-stopping high tenor voices of Clyde McPhatter, Dee Clark, and Ted Taylor;
* Jimmy Reed with his harmonica strapped to his neck, singing and playing guitar with a seemingly liquid motion and a singular, sweeping sound;
* The ability of the Platters to take a fun-loving teenage rock and roll audience and hush them with their music to the point that one could hear the proverbial pin drop;
* The powerful voice and sexy tease of Lavern Baker;
* The unique single string guitar of Californian Duane Eddy;
* The zany antics and surprisingly sharp harmonies of the Coasters;
* The voice and unabashed talent of the greatly underrated Ruth Brown;

41

* The hilarious comedy of emcee **Clay Tyson;**
* The surprising talent of **Bobby Rydell;**
* The requisite saxophone solos by the backup orchestras;
* The booming voice of **Big Joe Turner;**
* The heavenly harmonies of the **Flamingos** and the **Moonglows;**
* The endless string of hits as sung by pioneering Atlantic Records' groups, the **Drifters** and the **Clovers;**
* The excitement of **James Brown and the Famous Flames.**

Then there was **Bo Diddley.** He was the consummate performer, yet totally unpredictable. During one show, he strode on-stage with a box-shaped guitar. In another, his sister played backup guitar. He was the first artist I ever saw use a remote control electric guitar, which freed him to roam into the audience. There was something special, almost mystical about Bo. The rich, full sound of his guitar literally filled an auditorium, sounding like twenty guitars playing in unison.

One evening as Bo was playing his new-fangled guitar during his performance, a couple of obnoxious rowdies were acting up in the front row of the auditorium. Bo slowly exited the stage, and positioned himself squarely in front of the two guys—deftly playing his guitar, never missing a beat. He stood over the mischief makers in that confident, almost cocky air which was his alone, not uttering a word, until the two quietly slunk back into their seats. The audience cheered lustily as Bo calmly and measurably strummed his way back to the stage, where he proceeded to deliver one hell of a performance.

Bo had a maracas player named Jerome Green—immortalized in the song "Bring It To Jerome." Jerome once boldly ventured out into the audience and began selling programs during the performances of the other acts. On occasion Jerome would sing along with Bo, as he did on Bo's biggest chart record, "Say Man." It was Jerome who served as Bo's raucous, jiving counterpart, and it featured the two playfully teasing and chiding each other to a driving Latin rhythm.

"Say man, you should be ashamed of yourself."
"Why?"
"Calling people ugly."
"I didn't call you ugly."
"What'd you say?"
"I said you was ruined, that's all."

42

The last time I saw Bo during his heyday was in the fall of 1962. He was on the bill with Jackie Wilson, the Four Seasons, Bobby "Blue" Bland, the Falcons, the Fiestas, and Bunker Hill, who had a jiving hit called "Hide And Go Seek." The Four Seasons had the hottest record in the country at the time, a monster hit entitled "Big Girls Don't Cry." Unfortunately they had not yet worked the song up for a live performance. The crowd was highly and vocally upset—and even booed the Four Seasons loudly. Bo was the next act and the crowd's lusty cat-calls drowned out Bo's introduction. Bo took the stage anyhow, coolly plugged in his equipment, then struck the first few hot riffs of his opener. The Bo Diddley beat and patented sound quickly turned the boos into rousing cheers. We quickly forgot all about the Four Seasons as Bo rocked the house.

Bunker Hill's rollicking performance that night was unique, to say the least. He strode onto the stage and took about ten one dollar bills from his pocket, dramatically crumpled them and threw each one into the frenzied crowd. Regardless, Bunker was one singer who knew how to get the audience up for his performance! The dizzying momentum he created was maintained through his act, and he left the crowd screaming and yelling for more.

7 Jackson, pp. 123-124.

CHAPTER 8

FOLK MUSIC ON CAMPUS

With mixed emotions, I watched the news of Elvis' induction into the army in 1958, my junior year in high school. I thought that, maybe, his overseas assignment would shift his popularity to my beloved R&B music and its artists. But, at the same time, I knew that rock and roll music could be hurt, especially R&B. After all, Elvis' popularity was the main catalyst in the overall popularity of rock and roll. Following the media coverage of the induction, his hair being cut, and so on, I developed a respect for Elvis as a citizen and human being. After all, he refused special privileges and demanded to be treated as any other enlisted man.

While Elvis was in the army in Germany, rock and roll did lose a little of its steam. The recording industry continued to sanitize the music by pushing the white teen idols and folk music—which were much less threatening than the black music that permeated rock and roll—of which Elvis was a part.

It was in the early summer of 1959, after my senior year that I started dating my first true love, Frankie Eassy, who was a cashier at the Carolina Theater, where I worked as a movie usher. We both loved our jobs, and even though the pay was minimal, we could see movies free of charge. As a bonafide movie freak that "bennie" more than made up for the low wages. The money we did earn gave us that much longed for taste of independence.

Frankie was genuinely sweet and very pretty. She had the most beautiful, deeply expressive eyes and when she looked at me I melted like butter! She was exceptionally quiet when I first met her, but soon

44

loosened up, and revealed a terrific sense of humor—even laughing at my corniest jokes! Nothing mattered to me except being with Frankie. Saying good-bye to her the night before I left for college was one of the most difficult tasks I've ever faced. "Guess Who," by Jesse Belvin was our special song, and we played it over and over again that last evening together. Talk about choked up. Whew! I just couldn't shake the uneasy feeling that, when I left Greenville to attend college, we would never make it together.

The summer of 1959 had been truly one of the happiest, best times of my life. And as that summer all too quickly faded away, my life path encountered a major fork in the road. As I was soon to learn, so had the path of rock and roll. It was the end to the decade I loved best, the 50's—and it was the end of innocence. My life, the music I loved, and society would soon be changed forever.

The drive to Columbia that steamy, hot September Sunday in my father's black 1949 Cadillac was one of the most depressing days of my life. Feeling totally alone, I ached for Frankie to be with me. I searched the car's radio dial for some rock and roll music, and there was none to be found. And to make matters worse, the car conked out on me 35 miles down the road.

At age 17, I simply was not ready for college. I had wanted to continue working, save money, open a mail order record shop like Randy's or Ernie's, and marry Frankie. But Dad wanted what was "best for me" and was paying for my college education. "Son, there'll be no arguments, you're going to have it better than I did. You are going to college." This mediocre student was heading off for the University of South Carolina, feeling unprepared, inadequate, and subconsciously ready to rebel against the system.

Arriving on the sprawling campus late that afternoon seemed like a scene from a movie. Thousands of students happily bustled about, like ants at a picnic, chattering and laughing amongst themselves. I felt pretty much out of place as it seemed that everyone knew one another and were already into their routines. There were good looking girls everywhere but none matched Frankie. However, the obvious buzz of excitement in the air temporarily lifted my spirits.

Not knowing what to expect and carrying a heavy load of rock

45

and roll records, I found my dorm room. When my roommate Alan Horne arrived, I knew right away that we would get along fine. He was a couple of years older than me and definitely marched to his own drummer. He was refreshing to be around, as almost everyone else was conformist to a fault.

With reluctance, Alan and I attended the required freshman orientation, where we were herded into the gym for our first taste of college life and initiation into the "privilege of becoming college men and women." After the ritual welcome by school administrators, we were introduced to the football cheerleaders who proceeded to teach us cheers for the up-coming football game. A perky, knockout blonde instructed the wide-eyed group emphatically by shaking her pompoms, "You yelled the word 'heck' in high school, but you're in college now, so from now on, the word you yell is 'hell!' " Most of the "liberated" freshmen excitedly shouted and whooped at the word "hell." Alan and I looked at each other and exclaimed in unison, "You've got to be kidding!"

Looking back, it reminds me of **The Buddy Holly Story**, where Buddy took his girlfriend to the bus to see her off to college. He had chosen that moment to tell her that he would not be going with her, and that he saw his future differently than hanging out with the college gang. She was horrified. "But," she stammered, "what will I tell the kids?" With the perfect tinge of disgust he replied, "Boolah Boolah."

College days have given many students their first taste of freedom. At home I had used Mother's car whenever I wanted it and was financially independent due to my job. Mother had rules, true, but was lenient and basically trusted Aubrey and me. My first taste at college was exactly the opposite of most students. There was no money and no car, so I felt less free and more confined than in Greenville.

Nonetheless, I found myself strongly pursued by Lambda Chi Alpha fraternity and joined, thus becoming a "fraternity pledge," despite Alan's exhortations against it. What about conformity? Learning my lessons the hard way, I moved into the fraternity house dorm and was sucked into the swirl of fraternity life. Fraternity pledges, I soon found out were treated like marine basic trainees, and were ordered to do a number of incredibly idiotic "duties." I knew I'd been had.

By November, I had broken up with Frankie. Jesse Belvin's "Guess Who" and those special times now seemed hauntingly long ago

46

and far away. My grades were going down the tube, and I was using every spare dime I had to play poker and pin ball machines. I had attended a "Biggest Show Of Stars" rock and roll concert in Columbia and was one of only about 200 in the audience, while the same show had been a sellout with 5000 attendees in Greenville. I felt terribly out of place at college and in a college town. To make things worse, the music on the radio in Columbia was terrible, and without a car, the most exciting thing to do on a date was walk to the student center and drink Cokes. Gee golly thunder whompers! Even going to football games was ruined because we were crammed in the middle of the student section like a bunch of sardines. I was the proverbial "bull in a china shop" with a bad attitude—for me, college life stunk. But with my rock and roll record collection and trusty old turntable, whenever college life got to me, I would put on a little Fats Domino and things suddenly seemed just a little better.

Luckily at school, I had developed a unique assortment of friends, and these relationships helped ease the down side of college life. Next to girls, music was the favorite topic. Lane Caughman would burst into my room after a night on the town and demand to hear some Fats Domino or Joe Turner. No matter what the hour, it was a request I couldn't turn down. Some of us even formed a kind of rock and roll rat pack and adopted artists' names as our nicknames. There were Marv (Johnson) Jordan, Fats (Domino) Caughman, Jimmy (Reed) Gamble, Bo (Diddley) Horne and Lloyd (Price) Turner. We spent hours listening to records, and playing our favorite artists. I had no idea that I would later come to know many of the artists adopted by the rat pack.

For the first semester, I stayed in the room next to Billy (Marv Johnson) Jordan. Dog tired from too much partying and trying to sleep one night, I heard Billy and his roommate laughing and talking—and the banter became louder and louder through the walls. A lusty "bull shit," was followed by an emphatic "horse shit," then a vociferous "owl shit," "rat shit," "turkey shit," "dog shit," and more laughter. The more I concentrated on sleeping, the more boisterous this little game became. Fighting mad because I had an exam the next day, I was "Tossin' and Turnin,'" as the hit goes by Bobby Lewis. Finally it got quiet—and I was almost asleep—when I was jerked awake by a bellowing "platypus shit." There was dead silence for several minutes followed by a sleepy "orangutan shit" and then dead silence again. By that time, to hell with sleep, I was laughing so hard, tears were streaming down my cheeks—and the next day I actually made a rare good grade on my English exam!

It soon became clear that many college students also had their own music, and it wasn't good-time rock and roll or R&B. Mother had told me a few years earlier, "You'll outgrow rock and roll when you mature." To many parents of the day, nothing personified immaturity more than rock and roll music. With that sage advice firmly implanted, I found out that sure enough, these "mature" college students had adopted a cooler, more serious, more intellectual, more "adult" music. It was also blander, duller and downright depressing to me. My mother's words made me think long and hard, as I noticed the acceptance and adoption of folk music as the music of choice among "in" college students.

This "hip" music was an offshoot of the music which flowed from tiny stages to smoke-filled rooms full of beatniks in coffee houses of Greenwich Village in New York. The music on campus was a little less "artsy" and a little more collegiate than that originating in "the village," but still a long, long way from good-time rock and roll. In 1959, the undisputed kings of folk music were the Kingston Trio. They had gotten their start at a San Francisco nightclub called The Hungry I. Trio members Bob Shane, Nick Reynolds and Dave Guard were collegiate to the bone, sporting pin-stripe, button-down collar shirts, trim haircuts, and an overall neat appearance. Their biggest hit was "Tom Dooley", a requisite anthem among 1959 college students. Other hits were "M.T.A.," "A Worried Man," "Scarlet Ribbons," "Scotch And Soda," and "Tijuana Jail." It seemed as if every student on campus had a Kingston Trio album, or at least a 45. That is, except me!

Another popular folk group of the time was the Brothers Four, whose hit, the mournful "Greenfields" was a smash on campus. They put on a free concert at the university field house and out of curiosity I took a date to hear them. Their performance was good as far as folk music goes, still I kept nodding off from lack of sleep caused by too many all night poker games. But I was jarred awake by the familiar refrains of a favorite rock and roll song, "Walking Along," the hit by both the Solitaires and the Diamonds. Only the Brothers Four weren't just singing, they were making fun of it by deliberately acting the part of drunken bums singing off key, out of harmony, and stumbling around instead of dancing. I was infuriated by this mocking of a good song as it only re-enforced the "better than thou" attitude folk music fans had toward "that high school rock and roll" which they had left behind.

Nationally, folk music was making certain inroads into rock and roll's dominance. This was encouraged by the major record label establishment, as most folk artists were on major labels. There was also a good bit of media publicity about the (hoped for) impending death of rock and roll. Many articles were written about Elvis being in the service in Germany and it was widely predicted that rock and roll would not survive his absence from the music scene. Parents also encouraged the acceptance of folk music because it was softer, and with the exception of Harry Belafonte and Josh White, more caucasian—thus safer.

Listening to the radio while downing my daily pimento cheese sandwich, it was reported that Elvis had returned from the service. Boy, was I happy to have him "Back In The U.S.A.," as echoed in the Chuck Berry song! I was glad when his straight to the heart rock and roll song— "Stuck On You," zoomed to number one on the charts—despite the naysayers. I hoped that he could help rekindle both the music and the spirit of the 50's which were slipping away before my eyes.

When fraternity and sorority parties were held, folk music was nowhere to be found. These very cool, aloof, folk music snobs, when loosened up, suddenly became wild, crazed, party animals dancing to my favorite R&B and good-time rock and roll songs. At one of those parties, Lambda Chi Alpha's Parisian Ball some of us pledges worked up a few skits. Unabashedly, I took the stage, did my impersonation of Chuck Berry while strumming a tennis racket, and lip synched his hit, "Maybelline." When I went into Chuck's patented "duckwalk," it brought the house down. Together with Billy Jordan and Bill Rast, we put on an energetic lip-synch rendition of the Coasters' hit "Young Blood." The crowd was wildly enthusiastic and loved it! Admittedly, so did we!

That night it became clear to me that the folk music craze was more trumped up than real, and would never become more than a secondary music force. And our skits showed that when the "supposed to" barriers were let down, rock and roll was still king. I remember thinking, "Mother—maybe, just maybe, my more serious, intellectual and mature college mates are simply playing a role and have not totally shed themselves of their pasts, after all."

The changes taking place in my life in the early 60's were as radical as the changes taking place in music as well as the very essence of society, and even politics.

There was a certain privileged phoniness about the whole John F. Kennedy presidential campaign, especially on campus. Most Kennedy supporters were those in the cool, folk music crowd, who seemed mainly awed by his looks, wealth and charisma. Several of my friends and I had worked diligently for Vice President Richard Nixon. The day after Kennedy was elected I remember being in a dejected state and hearing news commentator Paul Harvey remarking that the election was so close that when Kennedy walked down the street he would know that every other person he passed voted against him.

Former President Dwight Eisenhower, a five-star general and war hero, had been a re-assuring, substantive presence. But the media regarded Eisenhower and his wife, Mamie, as not very interesting and "just plain folks." The Nixons were viewed in much the same light.

Michelle Phillips of the 60's singing group, the Mamas and Papas writes in **California Dreamin'**[8]. "Unless you were a real asshole, you were on the side of the angels, of those who were always liberals. Here was a new young President with new young ideas . . . Richard Nixon, the Nightmare Man, who had lost the election so deservedly, [was] now a forgotten man with his deadly dull republican companions and supporters . . ."

Just as the record industry hyped the teen idols, the media began fawning over every move in "Camelot." They spent as much time following Kennedy's personal life as they did his politics, leading to the view worldwide that the Kennedys were America's "royalty." The nightly TV news became nightly Kennedy worship services! Kennedy became the first president created and glamorized by the media, thanks largely to his millionaire father, Ambassador Joseph P. Kennedy's influence and manipulation.

Kennedy was a fiscal conservative and tough in foreign policy. But he had a daring, almost reckless devil-may-care attitude, much like his favorite fictional character, James Bond, with whom he was often identified. Bond was the new breed hero—sexy, dashing, worldly and the epitome of cool, and his films were filled with buxom, sex goddesses. Bond got the bad guys, but viewed it as an irritant, so he could get on

50

with living for the moment. Humility was not in his vocabulary. This was a far cry from my all-American, rock-solid, substantive type hero, personified by John Wayne, whose movie characters treated women with respect, were rebellious in their own ways, but put their lives on the line to get the bad guys because of principle. Unlike me, many young people delighted in the hip new image that Bond and the new President represented. The ideals embodied in Wayne and Eisenhower were becoming passe—because they weren't sexy and glamorous enough for rebellious, living-on-the-edge kids. This blind, mindless support of Camelot made me uneasy, though I couldn't put my finger on exactly why, that Kennedy was not all that he appeared to be—and wishing that the simpler 50's were back.

In the same manner, big band music, R&B and original rock and roll were on balance cleaner, sweeter, more innocent and fun-filled, yet substantive music types—and representative of pre-60's ethics. The music of the teen idols (and the music to follow) however, was sex appeal driven, as was much of the appeal of Bond and Kennedy. It was suddenly clear to me that to both the media and the entertainment industry, sex appeal was rapidly becoming more important than character and substance.

I resigned from the fraternity and improved my grades somewhat over the next couple of semesters, but my enthusiasm for college had not budged one notch. Then I contracted mononucleosis and missed so many classes that I was forced to drop out of school. I returned to Greenville and took a job with the highway department as an inspector at an asphalt plant. The plant was located near a honky tonk beer joint called The Silver Dollar, where we sometimes dropped by after work for a beer.

I had often dreamed of becoming a singer so I jumped at the chance to substitute one evening as lead singer for a band which consisted of some old high school friends. The venue? The Silver Dollar, of course! The gritty, hard-drinking, hard-living country and western crowd must have cracked up over my soulful but misplaced performance. They loved the songs by Fats Domino, Chuck Berry, and Elvis, but otherwise, we could have been from another planet compared to this country crowd. Boy, I sure did sweat that night! It got even worse when Richard Brassell, the drummer, attempted to croon several Dean Martin songs.

The crowd heckled and hooted, as "Return To Me" and "Volare" were poles apart from honky tonkin' country music. The night could not have ended soon enough. So much for my singing career!

It was back to campus for me in the fall of 1961, and I realized even more than ever that college life just wasn't for me. I felt that I was on the proverbial slow boat to China without a rudder. So at semester's end my life took a radical turn as I decided to join the Air Force.

8 Michelle Phillips, *California Dreamin'* (New York, 1986). pp. 19-20.

CHAPTER 9

THE WILD BLUE YONDER

As changes in the fabric of life were gradually occurring, there were few more harsh for me than the change from civilian to military life. Arriving at Lackland Air Force Base in San Antonio, Texas in the wee hours of that cold, January 1962, morning, we were herded to a waiting area. I could faintly hear some of my favorite songs playing over a radio in the background. It was comforting to hear "Hey Baby" by Bruce Channel, "Let Me In" by the Sensations, and "Smoky Places" by the Corsairs in such an apprehensive situation.

From that moment it was, "Move! Move! Move!" Our steely-eyed TI's, were relentless to malingerers, goof-offs, and overweight trainees. The occasional breaks from the rigorous routine found me at canteens on the base where there were juke boxes. The usual lack of change didn't stop me from dropping quarters into the slot and selecting songs like "Love Letters" by Ketty Lester, "Good Luck Charm" by Elvis Presley, "Slow Twistin'" by Chubby Checker, "Dream Baby" by Roy Orbison or "Mashed Potato Time" by Dee Dee Sharp. Even the torture of basic training couldn't keep me from getting my fix! It was the most demanding eight weeks of my life. The experience did me a lot of good, if only for the discipline; but to be candid, I would not enjoy having to go through it again.

That summer found me transferred to Russian language school at Syracuse University in Syracuse, N.Y. at "Skytop." It was beautiful in upstate New York, and I was really feeling good, because I was "free" again, compared to basic training days. And as the months passed, there was a real camaraderie that embraced Syracuse during the snowy, winter months, especially in the neighborhood bars around the city. We frequented a quaint, little bar called The White Front, partly because of its proximity to school, but mostly for its ambiance. I must have played "Stand By Me" by Ben E. King over one hundred times on the juke box during our visits. There was a genuine friendliness and an ease that people showed each other that I have never felt anywhere since.

My turntable and records accompanied me to Syracuse and I was surprised at how many of the guys enjoyed my records. It even helped break the ice with the most serious and studious student in our class. Steve Weiss was the only Jewish guy and the only Californian, and he stayed pretty much to himself. While playing "Don't Drop It" by Wilbert Harrison one evening, there was a knock on my door. Steve, grinning widely, told me that "Don't Drop It" was his all time favorite record, as it had been a big hit in L.A. and he had not heard it in years. We became fast friends, and it even loosened him up among the other guys. It was a ritual for Steve to ask for Wilbert Harrison's song a couple of times every week.

Ed Welgat from Illinois and I even tried entertaining the guys with our amateurish duets of "All I Have To Do Is Dream" by the Everly Brothers, "I Understand" by the G-Clefs and "What's Your Name" by Don and Juan. And I do stress, amateurish!

Syracuse radio stations were playing the teenage idol schlock of the day, promulgated by American Bandstand, so my records gave them a much preferred alternative. The main stations were WNDR-AM and WOLF-AM. WOLF-AM was the station that, ironically, had given Dick Clark some of his radio experience, a few years earlier. It was obvious that the music was programmed almost exclusively to young girls. And by this time any music aimed at teenagers was classified as rock and roll. But there was a real incongruity in classifying the syrupy ballad "My Dad" by Paul Petersen in the same category as the rocking "Quarter To Three" by Gary "U.S." Bonds or its sound-a-like, "Runaround Sue" by Dion.

Music historians, mostly British, seem to conclude that rock and roll was in the doldrums from 1960 until 1964. Their judgment, no doubt, is based on the most actively promoted music of the time, teen idol music. But on the whole their judgment simply is not true. Most ingredients of early rock and roll were still prominent, but violins and other instruments had been added to the mix for a rich, orchestral sound and millions of records were being sold. The American music scene was actually vibrant and there were good reasons. For one, it was the era of the girl groups and female singers which included:

"Will You Love Me Tomorrow" The Shirelles
"Soldier Boy" The Shirelles
"Dedicated To The One I Love" The Shirelles
"He's So Fine" The Chiffons
"One Fine Day" The Chiffons
"Leader Of The Pack" The Shangri-Las
"My Boyfriends Back" The Angels
"He's A Rebel" The Crystals
"Da Doo Ron Ron" The Crystals
"Then He Kissed Me" The Crystals
"Be My Baby" The Ronettes
"Heat Wave"-Martha and the Vandellas
"Please Mr. Postman"-The Marvelettes
"Playboy"-The Marvelettes
"The One Who Really Loves You"-Mary Wells
"You Beat Me To The Punch"-Mary Wells
"Walk On By"-Dionne Warwick
"It's My Party"-Lesley Gore
"Ride"-Dee Dee Sharp
"Locomotion"-Little Eva
"Party Lights"-Claudine Clark
"Gee Whiz"-Carla Thomas
"You'll Lose A Good Thing"-Barbara Lynn
"Just One Look"-Doris Troy
"I Know"-Barbara George
"Mama Didn't Lie"-Jan Bradley

Then there was producer Phil Spector and his "wall or sound." Overdubbing techniques and echoes, combined with a number of singers and musicians, made it sound like a wall of sound was aimed straight at the listener. In addition to the Crystals and the Ronettes, Spector also produced the Alley Cats, Darlene Love, Bob B. Soxx and the Blue Jeans, and his biggest stars, the Righteous Brothers. The Spector sound was infectious, and had a soulful feel through and through. This unique sound can best be found in "Puddin' N' Tain"-the Alley Cats, "Zip A Dee Doo Dah"-Bob B. Soxx and the Blue Jeans, "You've Lost That Lovin' Feelin'"-

the Righteous Brothers and "Be My Baby,"-the Ronettes.

There was not much R&B to be found on Syracuse radio, other than records that were showing up on the national music charts. Some of my service buddies and I found a cozy, candle-lit restaurant called Luigi's Italian Village, which featured a lively R&B combo. So at least once a week, Dick Verciglio, Vern Moreland, Doug Diggle, Alan Mowbray, Robert Spooner, Charles McCullough and I were there. We had a ball, drinking, laughing, talking, listening and dancing to the R&B music of Herb "Ebbtide" Nelson on organ and Art "Legs" Robbins on vocals. Chuck Jackson's "Any Day Now" and the Drifters' "Up On The Roof" were favorites that we requested again and again.

At Skytop one of my best friends was a witty, crazy guy named Jim Prather who was a big music fan. His favorites were Bo Diddley and the Platters. There was never a dull moment with Jim! We secured a three-day pass and took a getaway trip to New York City one week-end. As we were ambling along near Roseland Ballroom looking at the sights, I spotted a gentleman that looked like Herb Reed, the bass singer of the Platters. I marched up to him, with Jim sheepishly in tow, and asked him if he were indeed Herb Reed. He answered affirmatively, and immediately smiled, turned and introduced us to their new lead singer, Sonny Turner.

Herb then related a story from one of their Canadian tours in the mid-50's when an awestruck young boy and his parents invited them to dinner. The boy proudly told him that he was going to be a rock and roll star in a few years. Herb remarked, "You know what? The boy was dead serious. His name was Paul Anka, and was he ever right!" It was a fascinating story and, the normally talkative, saucer-eyed Jim was rendered speechless by this chance meeting with a few of his favorite artists and the stories we heard. For us both, it was truly a small world.

Chattering away about the Platters, Jim and I continued our sightseeing. Despite the bustling activity on the sidewalk, Jim spotted a driver struggling to parallel park and quickly offered his assistance. With crystal clear directions, Jim directed and motioned with his hands "Turn your wheels one more time. That's right! Now to the left, back up, and . . . you're in!" The man threw up his hands and with a heavy Brooklyn accent, barked, "Get in? Damn it, ya idiot, can't ya see I'm tryin' to get out?" Jim, red-faced, just turned and walked away. After recovering from

56

a fit of laughter I began singing the lyrics from the Lavern Baker song, "Jim Dandy," except it was Jim Prather to the <u>rescue</u>.

Jim died unexpectedly one icy New Year's Eve a decade later from a cerebral hemorrhage, but I will always have many fond memories of Jim, his wife Lorraine and the times we had together.

The folk music movement had begun to pick up steam in 1962 with the popularity of Peter, Paul, and Mary. Their hits, such as "Blowin' In The Wind," "Puff The Magic Dragon," and "If I Had A Hammer" were extremely popular. Other artists of the time were the Chad Mitchell Trio, the Brothers Four, the New Christy Minstrels, Joan Baez, Judy Collins, the Rooftop Singers, and the "old" standbys, the Kingston Trio. Some of my "cooler" Air Force friends like Charles McCullough got into it big time, but they continued to like rock and roll as well. Folk music was popular mainly on college campuses, but, due to a television show, "Hootenanny," was beginning to broaden and grow. Hosted by Jack Linkletter, it featured folk performers in a more good-time atmosphere than the traditional beatnik, coffee house setting. I watched it occasionally, but could get nowhere near the enjoyment that I did from shows that featured rock and roll.

Hank Ballard and the Midnighters had been together since the early 50's and were considered to be the ultimate party group. Their hits, such as "Work With Me Annie," "Annie Had A Baby," "Sexy Ways," and "Get It" were jukebox classics. In 1959, Hank released what was to become an historic 45 rpm record. The A side was titled "Teardrops On Your Letter," and became a moderate hit. The B side became a number one record on the charts in my hometown, Greenville, S.C., but was only a moderate hit nationwide. It would bear the name of one of the biggest dance crazes in history, "The Twist."

But it was a former chicken plucker from Philadelphia who would turn "The Twist" into a household word. Ernest Evans had previously had a minor hit called "The Class," on which he sang "Mary Had A Little Lamb" imitating Fats Domino, Elvis Presley, the Coasters and others. Dick Clark's wife had seen him perform and said that he reminded her of Fats Domino; like a "Chubby Checker." He readily adopted the name, as Fats was his idol. Chubby's version of "The Twist" was almost an exact copy of Hank's, but the exposure it received on American Bandstand sent it to the number one position on the national record charts. Hank laughingly remarked, "Harry, Chubby even copied my 'Eee-ohs'." It became the only record in history by the same artist to hit number one in consecutive years.

In 1961, a night spot in New York City, the Peppermint Lounge, featured the rock and roll group, Joey Dee and the Starliters. When newspapers printed photos of some New York society types doing the twist to Joey's music, the Peppermint Lounge became the "in" place to be in New York, and the twist the "in" dance. Its fame soon spread nationwide and the twist craze was on its way. The twist was the first dance that was embraced by adults, as well as teenagers. When it was reported that President Kennedy, First Lady Jackie and other members of Camelot were avid "twisters," nothing could stop it.

Joey recorded "The Peppermint Twist," and it soon reached the top of the record charts. Suddenly everybody, from Sam Cooke to Gary "U.S." Bonds, was recording "twist" records, which became hits. Its peak of popularity lasted only two to three years, but, even today, it is played wherever people dance. Because of their association with the twist, Chubby and Joey are still going strong in the 90's.

After the twist's success, numerous other good-time dances and hit records sprang up that bore their names. The Watusi, the Pony, the Swim, the Monkey, the Hully Gully, the Jerk, the Mashed Potatoes, the Boogaloo, the Popeye, and the Shimmy, Shimmy were but a few. Dance partners stood opposite each other and moved in unison without touching. Until this time, most dances featured either an embrace of sorts, or at least hand holding. I still preferred the shag, but did enjoy the songs that went with these new dances.

In Detroit, Michigan, a budding record industry entrepreneur was beginning to make some musical noise. Berry Gordy, Jr. had written and produced a few records, mainly for Jackie Wilson and Marv Johnson in the late 50's. He had established his own record label, Tamla, but since it was under-financed, was forced to give early distribution rights to other labels such as United Artists. Marv told me during the 80's about the first Motown recording (Tamla 101-Marv's "Come To Me"): "I would be exaggerating and complimentary to say it was done on a shoe string budget." By the early 60's, Berry was able to strengthen his financial position and began to release and distribute all material on his own labels. Bingo! It happened with Barrett Strong, Smokey Robinson and the Miracles, and

Mary Wells, as they scored on his labels with "Money," "Shop Around," and "Bye Bye, Baby," respectively. In 1961, the Marvelettes had the first national number one hit for any of Berry's labels. It was released and nationally distributed on the same label, Tamla (now properly financed) that had started with Marv Johnson. That number one hit was "Please Mr. Postman." As I was making my way through my early Air Force days, Gordy's Motown momentum was building.

Upon graduation from our Russian language course we were transferred to Goodfellow Air Force Base, in San Angelo, Texas in the spring of 1963. It was an intense, grueling three months learning Russian voice interception. But what made it almost unbearable was the weather. The intense heat and dryness of the area almost seared our lungs. Non-stop dust storms blew sand in our eyes and mouths. There were no trees for shade and our barracks were not air-conditioned. If it hadn't been for good ole' R&B music and Airman Dodge, I'm not sure I could have made it . . .

Two rock and roll shows came to the local coliseum while we were stationed there. The first show featured Chubby Checker, the Fiestas, and the Falcons and turned out to be a sham. I had seen both the Fiestas and the Falcons a few months earlier in Greenville, and knew immediately that these were bogus groups. Then out came Chubby Checker, thin as a rail and sounding more like a screech owl than Chubby. Unfortunately, the artists skipped out before anybody could do anything about it. A near riot ensued, but San Angelo's rock and roll fans had been taken for a ride that evening.

This debacle was fresh in the minds of us fans, so we plunked down our money to see the Bo Diddley show with some trepidation. We were guaranteed that it would be the real Bo Diddley. The audience buzzed with excitement as the enthusiastic emcee built up Bo's introduction. The band was playing, but . . . there was no Bo. Shifting in our seats nervously, we were thinking that we had been "taken" again. Suddenly the main spotlight shot to the back of the auditorium, and we turned and gasped at the sight of . . . Bo Diddley in a brilliant red jacket! Deftly strumming his guitar, he made his way through the relieved and wildly, cheering crowd. What a show he put on that night!

I'm reminded of Bo's hit, "Say Man" when I think of my buddy (and country music fan) Airman Richard Dodge who was constantly stir-

59

ring things up. Much like Bo and Jerome in "Say Man," he was always jiving. His pet saying was, "You can't bull shit the bull shitter." Dodge loved calling out someone's name and when they answered, shooting back, "Never mind, just checking ass holes." No one could ever pay him back until ...

One morning we were lined up for parade review and I was standing next to the lieutenant who was leading our flight. He was unbelievably serious and deadpan. An idea hit me, but it involved the lieutenant. I wasn't sure that he had a human side, much less a sense of humor, but I got his attention and told him my idea. After a moment of silence, he barked out an order for the flight to come to attention. We snapped to immediately. In a loud booming voice, the lieutenant roared "Airman Dodge!" Dodge replied, "Yes sir!" The stone-faced lieutenant retorted, "Never mind, just checking ass holes!" Pandemonium broke loose, and later that day Dodge came up to me, haltingly broke into a grin, shook my hand, and, without a word, walked away. Say man!

With Phil Spector's "wall of sound," the girl groups, many talented female singers, the twist and other dances, folk music and the hootenanny, and the budding Motown sound, the American music scene was alive and well during the early 60's. Those British music critics who deride it suffer from shortsightedness, caused by their almost exclusionary affinities for the music and artists from the British-influenced "rock" scene.

CHAPTER 10

THE BEATLES CHANGE IT ALL

U.S. Air Force Security Service Headquarters at Kelly Air Force Base, San Antonio, Texas, was where I spent the rest of my service career. It was also where I experienced the beginning of a fundamental change in the fabric of popular music.

Not long after my arrival I began to hear about a rock and roll group that was causing quite a stir in Europe. The group was from England, and I didn't give it much thought, because English rock and roll artists and their music were considered vastly inferior to what was generated at home. The most notable English rock and roller at the time was Cliff Richards, and he had made hardly a dent in the U.S.

The group did not even fare well when one of their records was reviewed on American Bandstand, during the late autumn of 1963. Dick Clark relates in his book, <u>Rock, Roll & Remember</u>⁹, a conversation with Bernie Binnick of Swan Records about the record, "She Loves You," and the reaction of those in the audience of American Bandstand: "Some of the kids snickered, others laughed at the picture of the four shaggy-haired boys from Liverpool. The response was less than enthusiastic. After the show I called Swan (record label). Bernie got on the phone. 'You saw?' 'yeah, . . . we may have a stiff,' said Bernie. 'Thanks for giving it a try anyway.'" The group was the Beatles.

As I began to hear more about the Beatles' overseas popularity, and their impending visit to the U.S., I wondered if they would have an impact on American music. I was aware of the Beatles' love for R&B and American good-time rock and roll and thought that, if they made a difference at all, it would probably drive folk music away, and only increase the influence of R&B-based music.

Changes were coming. It was mid-afternoon Friday, November 22, 1963 and we were working in our office when a breathless, pale-faced tech sergeant burst in to tell us that President Kennedy had just been shot in Dallas. I had seen the Kennedys in a motorcade near the base just the day before, and couldn't believe it. Soon after, the radio reported that he had been pronounced dead. Most of us reacted with stunned silence but, to my surprise, a couple of guys in the office cheered.

The media, with round-the-clock coverage of the unfolding events, gave the impression that the country had stopped functioning. But that evening Ray Lemmons and I attended a Brackenridge High football game to watch their amazing running back Warren McVea. The atmosphere was somewhat subdued, but it was the usual-sized crowd. When the National Football League games were played that Sunday afternoon, I was glad. But I felt guilty for wanting a break from constant replay of news of the people weeping in the streets, and wondered if my friends and I were the only ones who felt that way. It was one of the most depressing week-ends I can ever remember, but I felt it was because the media used Kennedy's death for non-altruistic purposes and helped put the country into a deeper state of mental depression than was necessary.

The assassination of Kennedy, who was many young peoples' infallible hero, was viewed as the fault of the adult establishment. Onto the scene bounded the four mop-headed Beatles from England. Appearing on The Ed Sullivan TV Show before a live audience of screaming young girls, it was like a "call to arms" for impressionable kids, even though rumor has it that many of the screaming girls were paid "plants." The "spontaneity" was well orchestrated—there were radio promos, billboards, bumper stickers and buttons all over the New York City metropolitan area proclaiming, "The Beatles Are Coming" for weeks before their New York arrival. A lady recently told me that there was so much advance publicity about the show that her church group was let out early so they could go home and watch Ed Sullivan, even though most of the kids didn't even have the slightest idea who the Beatles were. She told me that ironically, it was also the first time she ever remembered that happening in her strict "Bible-belt" Baptist church.

Several of us Airmen were watching the TV show in the barracks' lounge, and we all were shaking our heads, laughing, and shouting cat calls. It reminded me of the hysteria over Fabian, and all of the guys watching the show viewed the Beatles on about the same level. The general consensus in the barracks was that it was mindless and very bubblegummish.

John Lennon, Paul McCartney, Ringo Starr, and George Harrison were truly the right people in the right place at the right time and had the right promotion-minded manager, Brian Epstein. The "fun-loving" Beatles literally swept kids out of their negative frames of mind. Because adults looked askance at the Beatles' long hair, and their music, what better way, was there for teenagers to express themselves than to wholeheartedly embrace this British group?

The American media were positive about the Beatles right from the start. David P. Szatmary in <u>Rockin' in Time</u>[10] explains: "<u>Newsweek</u> probably best captured the majority opinion when it labeled the Beatles 'a band of evangelists. And the gospel is fun. They shout, they stomp, they jump for joy and their audiences respond in a way that makes an old-time revival meeting seem like a wake . . . The Beatles appeal to the positive, not negative. They give kids a chance to let off steam and adults a chance to let off disapproval. They have even evolved a peculiar sort of sexless appeal: cute and safe . . .'" The emphasis, like American rock and roll, was on fun. There was a certain innocence about the long-haired groups from across the Atlantic Ocean. What teenager's mother couldn't find something lovable about these non-threatening British kids?

The Beatles had gained popularity in Europe by doing inferior versions of American rock and roll. Listen to the Beatles singing "Please Mr. Postman," "Roll Over Beethoven," "Chains," or "Money." When comparing their versions to the originals by the Marvelettes, Chuck Berry, the Cookies, and Barrett Strong, the Beatles' were not in the same league with the American artists'. "Twist And Shout" was their best cover record, but I'll take the Isley Brothers' original version any day. The Beatles were doing nothing more than a repeat of what happened in the 50's. Their versions of original American music, were no better than Pat Boone's versions of Fats Domino and Little Richard a decade earlier.

In the book <u>Blown Away</u>[11] by A. E. Hotchner, Atlantic Records' President Ahmet Ertegun described the black influence in the Beatles' early recordings, ". . . their first records were Chuck Berry songs; they sounded pretty ratty as a band, but that black influence came through very strongly."

Why did this move with the Beatles toward glitz and glamour happen? It had been picking up steam since Elvis and the teen idols of the late 50's. Millions of pre-teen and teen females had developed crushes on individual Beatles, so any critical examination was cast aside as the public was engulfed in a tidal wave of hype. Their popularity was so strong that quality did not even enter the equation.

The record industry quickly embraced any group of long-haired British youngsters. Like the Beatles, how they sounded mattered very little. If they fit the "image," all they had to be was adequate musically. Following on the heels of the Beatles were numerous British acts and the "British Invasion" was now under way. Some examples and their hits were:

The Dave Clark Five-"Glad All Over," "Bits And Pieces," "Can't You See That She's Mine," "Because," "I Like It Like That," "Catch Us If You Can," "Over And Over"

The Animals-"House Of The Rising Sun"

The Rolling Stones-"Time Is On My Side," "The Last Time," "Satisfaction," "Get Off Of My Cloud"

Gerry and the Pacemakers-"Don't Let The Sun Catch You Crying," "How Do You Do It?," "Ferry Cross The Mersey"

Freddie and the Dreamers-"I'm Telling You Now"

Billy J. Kramer and the Dakotas-"Little Children," "Bad To Me"

Herman's Hermits-"Can't You Hear My Heartbeat," "Mrs. Brown You've Got A Lovely Daughter," "Silhouettes," "Wonderful World," "I'm Henry VIII, I Am," "Just A Little Better"

The Kinks-"You Really Got Me," "All Day And All Of The Night," "Tired Of Waiting For You"

Peter and Gordon-"A World Without Love," "I Go To Pieces"

Manfred Mann-"Do Wah Diddy Diddy"

Wayne Fontana and the Mindbenders-"Game Of Love"

The Yardbirds-"For Your Love," "Heart Full Of Soul"

American radio stations began carrying top ten countdowns of what was popular in England, and suddenly what British rock and roll fans liked became more important than what fans in the United States liked. The country that invented rock and roll was now playing second fiddle to England. Since that time what British fans, performers and critics think has continued to have a mammoth influence on rock and roll here in the U.S.

The British Invasion consisted not only of English acts but eventually of American acts who copied the English sound. The groups were very young and white, and the singers' voices had little depth of feeling or soul. Saxophones, horns and pianos, key instruments of American R&B and rock and roll, were almost non-existent. The Beatles' instrumentation consisted of two electric guitars, an electric bass, and a set of drums. And as acts copied the Beatles, they also copied their instrumentation. From the mid-60's on, rock and roll became guitar dominated.

More importantly, the groups were musically self-contained. Before the British Invasion most acts were not. Steve Charles, black former lead singer with the R&B group the Clovers, was lead vocalist with white instrumental groups in the late 60's. He explained to me, "Black instrumentalists were considered superior to whites in rock and roll before the British Invasion, and British groups playing their own instruments made it all right to be white."

Self-contained groups were cost effective, but the concentration of musical talent was greatly diluted. When Sam Cooke, for instance, performed and recorded, he was backed by professional musicians with a large variety of instruments and background vocalists. The level of quality can be equated with the earlier, more detailed Snow White animated cartoon as compared to the later, more abstract Mr. Magoo type. Was I the only fan who noticed the change in rock and roll's quality?

When the British Invasion first began, my friends and I thought that it was kind of amusing, but we never viewed it as good music. We thought that it would simply be a fad and that the R&B-based music that we loved best would re-establish its pre-British Invasion position of strength. At the very least we felt that it would co-exist with American good-time rock and roll.

The British Invasion did not dominate in the Southeast as it did in most of the U.S. While San Antonio's top radio stations were saturating the air waves with British music in 1964, my sister Aubrey sent me a top 40 chart from a top Greenville, S.C. radio station, WQOK. It was dominated by the likes of Marvin Gaye, the Temptations, Otis Redding, Barbara Lewis, the Tams, the Drifters, etc. R&B was still firmly entrenched back home, and it took a pretty good while for British music

65

to gain a strong foothold in the Southeast. The attitude there was, "If I can't shag or bop to it, then don't play it for me."

The pockets of resistance, such as the music fans in the Carolinas and the Southeast, were apparently not numerous enough to have made a difference to the recording industry. I feel a strong sense of regret about the rush the industry made to record anything British sounding. Suddenly, R&B, rockabilly, teen idol, folk, popular, rock and roll, and other diverse American artists found themselves with one thing in common—they were without recording contracts. In the recording industry, loyalties were shallow, and hype and catering to the fickle teen and female market became everything. For fans like me, it was just "tough luck."

Most of the public did not know it at the time, but the Beatles were anything but innocent, fun-loving lads from Liverpool. They were from working-class backgrounds and rock and roll was their way out. They had been performing for several years before they came to America, and were worldly beyond their years.

The major change in rock and roll came about when the Beatles shrewdly sought to expand their audience to include adults. Their popularity alone guaranteed them the luxury of mammoth record sales, regardless of content, so it was easy to experiment—because they had nothing to lose. So they recorded several songs with adult appeal and two of them written by Paul became immensely popular, "Yesterday" and "Michelle." They were songs even Frank Sinatra could perform. Actually, the songs were mournful-sounding folk style ballads. More important to note—certain "stodgy" music critics praised these efforts. The "Fab Four" were beginning to shed the image of a shallow, teeny-bopper rock and roll group.

Some of my older Air Force mates in their thirties and forties who had derided the Beatles when they first appeared on Ed Sullivan, now praised them—but only after the critical acceptance of their "new" music. This puzzled me because friends my age continued to feel as I did that from the standpoint of what we knew as rock and roll, the Beatles' music was inferior. The acceptance of "Yesterday" and "Michelle" fostered adult acceptance of the Beatles and rock and roll, but also forever altered the definition of rock and roll that millions of teenagers like me grew up with—fun-filled, R&B-based rock and roll. It was also the subtle begin-

66

ning of youth influence on adults—if the youthful Beatles could be taken seriously, so could young people in general. In truth, the "rabble rousers of rebellion" had sold out to the very establishment at whom teens aimed their rebellion. It was with mixed emotions that teenagers watched their parents accept the Beatles.

The next big British act was the Rolling Stones, a blues based group that was the epitome of outrageousness. We service guys thought the Rolling Stones were dirty and scruffy, but that their music was more palatable than most British groups. Perhaps the Beatles were forced to push the limits of their own behavior to stave off the advances the Stones were beginning to make into their territory.

A. E. Hotchner, in **Blown Away**[12] writes, "Although these rebellious teenagers had at first fastened their allegiance onto the Beatles, they reluctantly began to desert them when their parents began to share their enthusiasm for the Fab Four, an unexpected development that blunted the edge of their rebelliousness. It was this ironic twist that induced teenagers to turn to the gamy newcomers, the Stones, of whom their parents would never approve. In fact, parents angrily disapproved and the more the Stones were reviled—the more they were busted for drugs and enmeshed in unsavory scandals—the more parents were outraged by them, and the better the kids liked them."

Sound Bites[13] author Albert Goldman tells of a **Rolling Stone** magazine article about the Rolling Stones that paints a telling portrait that was unknown by most fans as the British influence progressed throughout the 60's: " . . . The picture that emerged of the rock establishment with its rapacious greed, its shifty, manipulative tactics, its utter unconcern for people's lives and decencies, and its incredible megalomania was worthy of a muckraking masterpiece on the Robber Barons.

. . . The new Robber Bands, make no mistake, come from England bent on crass exploitation. Anyone who has traveled with these musicians or simply sat for an afternoon in their dressing rooms can testify to the contemptuous and paranoid view they hold of this country. 'Grab the money and run' is their basic philosophy . . . the freebooting of these rock bandits ought to end forever the idea that the counterculture is founded on some genuine ethical ideal, or that it marks in any significant way a break with the prevailing capitalistic system."

My roommate, Dave Seabury and I, went to see a movie that

vividly illustrated the differences between American and British music . Called the T.A M.I . (Teenage Awards Music International) show, it featured the Miracles, the Rolling Stones, Marvin Gaye, Gerry and the Pacemakers, the Supremes, Chuck Berry, Jan and Dean, Lesley Gore, and James Brown among others. Because the Rolling Stones were the "hottest" act on the show, there was an assumption that they must also be the best. Their sneering, pouty lead singer, Mick Jagger, had already developed quite an ego. On the T.A.M.I. show, the Stones followed James Brown. Brown definitely kicked the Stones' butts that evening with an obviously superior performance, which noticeably frustrated the sweating Jagger, who clumsily attempted to match Brown's showmanship.

In his book, <u>The Death Of Rhythm & Blues</u>[14], Nelson George related that the T.A.M.I. audience consisted primarily of white teenage girls, and that there was constant screaming regardless of who was on stage. ". . . That they could cheer as Mick Jagger jiggled across the stage doing his lame funky chicken after James Brown's incredible, camel-walking, proto-moonwalking, athletically daring performance—greeting each with equal decibels—revealed a dangerous lack of discrimination. To applaud black excellence and white mediocrity with the same vigor is to view them as equals, in which case the black artist in America always loses."

Mick Jagger may have harbored a deep resentment against American rock and roll ever since. From the Atlanta <u>Journal-Constitution</u>[15], Sunday, November 19, 1989, comes a revealing side of Jagger as he talks about it. "On early rock 'n' roll: 'I Can't stand it. I never listen to Elvis Presley, Chuck Berry, Carl Perkins or any of that team. I can't bear all those people.'"

The T.A.M.I. movie clearly spelled the death knell for the days of British acts performing on the same stage with exciting American performers, black or white. Along with the world, we clearly witnessed that the Rolling Stones were not in the same class with James Brown. From then on, American acts on the same bill with British acts increasingly became non-threatening, though talented, laid-back blues or folk performers.

From then on British Invasion fans would have little opportunity to see original American rock and rollers on the same bill with British acts. Also, there was not a chance that America's golden music fans like my friends and I would spend $3.00 to see British acts like the Rolling Stones, as we felt they weren't good enough to make the effort. Had they, however, been on a show with an artist like Jackie Wilson we would have paid to see Jackie, and <u>may</u> have stayed to watch the Stones. This was the beginning of the separation of music types within rock and roll.

And yet, through it all, John Lennon never lost his love and appreciation for America's golden music. Shortly before he died, he recorded an album, "John Lennon/Rock and Roll," that went back to his roots. <u>The Lives Of John Lennon</u>[16] author, Albert Goldman reveals, ". . . there has never been a rocker who wasn't haunted by the thought that nothing has ever surpassed the original rock and roll."

<u>Lennon Companion</u>[17] edited by Elizabeth Thomson and David Gutman, an article by Lloyd Rose-"Long gone John: Lennon and the revelations", reprinted from the Boston <u>Phoenix</u>, further talks about the album: ". . . it's poorly produced; Lennon isn't in good voice; it's spiritless . . . It's hard to listen to it without the sinking feeling that he really believed 'Be-bop-a-lula' was greater than anything he'd ever written . . ." In a candid 1971 interview with Jann S. Wenner for <u>Rolling Stone</u>, Lennon confessed that, for him, there was nothing like the original rock and roll.

9 Dick Clark and Richard Robinson, *Rock, Roll & Remember* (New York, 1976). p. 252.

10 Szatmary, p. 119.

11 A.E. Hotchner, *Blown Away* (New York, 1990). p. 64.

12 Ibid., p. 38.

13 Albert Goldman, *Sound Bites* (New York, 1992). pp. 173-174.

14 George, p. 92.

15 Staff and Wire Reports, "Mick Jagger On His life As a Rocker." Atlanta *Journal-Constitution*, November 19, 1989. p. L1.

16 Albert Goldman, *The Lives Of John Lennon* (New York, 1988). p. 463.

17 Elizabeth Thomson and David Gutman. *Lennon Companion* (New York, 1987). p. 12.

CHAPTER 11

SOUL MUSIC AND THE BRITISH INVASION

In San Antonio, Texas, it was all but impossible for us enlisted guys to get a date with nice, civilian girls, because of the sheer number of service people in the area. We lived an existence of being "across the tracks," or, from the words of a Mills Brothers song, "Across The Alley From The Alamo."

Luckily, there were occasions to see various national artists. Concerts by Ray Charles, Chuck Berry, and Benny Goodman come to mind. But my favorite hang-out was The Eastwood Country Club, which provided some memorable entertainment. Most of the patrons were black, but there were quite a few whites as well, including a cadre of Air Force guys, led by yours truly.

The Eastwood had its regular performers. Miss Wiggles, the exotic dancer, could contort her body into shapes that seemed humanly impossible, while patrons watched with mouths agape. Curly Mays played a guitar—with his teeth! And the most well-known of the openers, Gatemouth Brown, had a winsome, folksy style to his blues.

But it was the headliners that could "kill" an audience. In fact, an incident at one of Bo Diddley's performances could have gotten us killed. My buddy Dave Seabury became highly irritated with dancers on the floor who were blocking Bo's performance. As he and a few others started loudly chanting, "Sit down!" "Sit Down!", pounding their fists on the table, I noticed a number of contemptuous stares directed our way, and felt more than a little uneasy. But much to my relief, other-patrons joined in with Dave, and the dancers were finally requested to sit down during the rest of Bo's show.

The electrifying Tina Turner and the Ikettes, with the shortest

70

sequined dresses and most beautiful, long, muscular legs I had ever seen, put on a dazzling dancing and singing show with "A Fool In Love" and other hits. Ike coolly played his guitar and stayed in the background like a perched hawk. Their presentation left us breathless and screaming for more.

But a particular performance by the Drifters one night blew me away totally. The group was in the middle of the Joe Tex hit, "Hold What You Got" when, suddenly, the lead singer collapsed on stage. We were thunderstruck, as all efforts to revive him failed. The other Drifters picked him up, and carried him off-stage to the dressing room, while we sat in stunned silence. Strangely enough, the band continued to play softly in the background when, all of a sudden, we heard a blood curdling scream. The "stricken" Drifter was running towards us, with the other Drifters in hot pursuit. He leaped onto the stage, landed on his knees, slid across the stage as he grabbed the mike, and continued singing in tempo with the music as the rest of the group joined him to finish the song. We gave them a rousing, though relieved, standing ovation. The whole thing had been totally staged and choreographed, and we fell for it all the way. It may have been hokey, but they pulled it off with total precision and drama.

It was while I was in the Air Force that R&B itself was undergoing a metamorphosis. At the decade's beginning, it consisted of a mix of doo-wop, New Orleans music, blues, spiritual music and novelty music. But as the 60's progressed there was an increasing emphasis on emotion and feeling—singing from the heart or soul—as influenced by Negro spirituals. So much R&B was recorded in this soulful style that it began to be referred to as "soul music," and R&B was sounding substantially different than in the 50's. And there was Motown.

The first distinctly soulful artist of the 60's was Solomon Burke, who came straight from the church, where, as a youngster, he had been known as "The Wonderboy Preacher." His first hit was in 1961 with a country and western flavored song, "Just Out Of Reach." Similar in background to Ivory Joe Hunter's 50's hit, "Since I Met You Baby," Burke's earthy delivery spoke volumes about soulful singing.

Then there was Wilson Pickett, former lead singer with the Falcons, whose trademark was his patented scream. Pickett possessed a boundless energy, and his songs were fun-filled, yet earthy. Only James

Brown exceeded Pickett as a shouting, screaming soul singer. Pickett was a favorite of mine right from the start.

The soul singer with the most class and charisma was Otis Redding. When I went home on leave my friends would play Otis Redding records ad infinitum, especially "Come To Me," and "These Arms Of Mine." Otis recorded for Stax/Volt out of Memphis, Tennessee, and was extensively promoted by his manager and friend Phil Walden. He gradually began to cross over to white audiences. Even so, at the time San Antonio stations seldom played Otis' hits, so I talked an Air Force buddy, Larry Brock into joining me at a downtown club to see this singer whom I talked about so effusively.

Otis gave a totally soulful, gut-wrenching performance that evening. I had known that he was somebody special, but that night proved it beyond a shadow of a doubt. There was a power to his music and in his performance that appealed to males in the audience, but he also exuded a certain charm and sex appeal that drove the women bananas.

What a talent we lost in that freezing lake near Madison, Wisconsin, when Otis and members of his band, The Bar-Kays, were tragically killed in an airplane crash carrying them to a concert in December of 1967. He had recorded "Sitting On The Dock Of The Bay" several days before his death and it went on to become his only number one record. I confess to having strong emotions every time I travel south to Macon, Georgia and cross the Otis Redding Memorial Bridge. It is a fitting tribute from his hometown to a man who gave so much, both to his community and to the world.

Then there was the Queen of soul music, Aretha Franklin. She was the daughter of a well-known black preacher from Detroit, Reverend C. L. Franklin. Aretha had been recording for several years for Columbia Records under the tutelage of people like Mitch Miller and her career had been undistinguished. She had put out good records, but the big band sound was too limiting for her massive voice and untapped talent. At a rock and roll concert in Greenville in the early 60's, though she was obviously talented, friends remarked while we watched her that her big band-style material was out of place with artists like Jackie Wilson and Sam Cooke.

Then, under the guidance of Atlantic Records' legendary producer, Jerry Wexler in 1967, Aretha took one of Otis' hits "Respect" and recorded it in her own style. Though Otis died a few months after Aretha scored with "Respect," he is reported to have commented that he may have written it, "but that it was Aretha's song now." She, of course, has gone on to become one of the biggest female singers in history.

Most of 60's soul music was recorded in Memphis, Tennessee, Muscle Shoals, Alabama or New York City. The driving forces were Jim Stewart and Al Bell in Memphis, Rick Hall in Muscle Shoals and Jerry Wexler in New York. Some of the songwriters included Isaac Hayes, Steve Porter, William Bell, Steve Cropper and Eddie Floyd. The more well-known musicians were Booker T. Jones, Steve Cropper, "Duck" Dunn, Willie Mitchell and Jimmy Johnson. There was a heavy emphasis on soulful singing and blaring horns. And although most of the singers were black, the songwriters and musicians were both black and white so the Memphis/Muscle Shoals soul sound was probably the most totally integrated popular music form in history.

The only major artist that was not a part of this connection was the King of Soul himself, James Brown. James had begun to hit it big after he recorded a live album "James Brown at The Apollo Theatre" on October 24, 1962. It is still considered to be one of the best live albums ever recorded. It went to number two on the pop chart and his stage show began touring extensively.

I first became tuned into the James Brown experience at a performance at a "Biggest Show Of Stars" concert in Austin, Texas. His show was well executed, highly energetic, and precision-tuned. His orchestra consisted of some of the best musicians anywhere. Since the driving back beat was of primary importance, it featured two drummers simultaneously.

As the audience anticipated the arrival of James Brown, the excitement would build to a crescendo. The announcer in his deep, strong voice enthusiastically shouted out a list of Browns' hits. Each hit mentioned was met with screams and applause. Finally with the audience anticipation at its apex, his voice boomed out, "And now, the star of the show, James Brown and the Fam-o-u-s Flames!"

The orchestra then shifted into a frenzy, and the unbelievable James Brown glided, slid, and danced across the stage! From that moment, he had the audience in the palm of his hands. He clutched,

73

caressed, and made love to the microphone, then turned, jumped, screamed, and danced, danced, danced as only he could. The whole thing was executed with such fury, yet with such grace and precision that it would boggle the mind of the uninitiated. My friends and I, clapping and yelling, never sat down once during his performance! The show's intensity continued until he broke into the strains and refrains of "Please, Please, Please." Falling to his knees, as if he could go no further, an assistant came out with a cape, placed it around his shoulders, and helped James to his feet. Drained, he slowly staggered to the side of the stage, with the assistant at his side. Then, as if struck by lightning, he began rapidly moving his legs up and down, and threw his cape aside. He then ran back, grabbed the mike, and again dropped to his knees, and squeezed every ounce of emotion possible out of the song. With the crowd cheering wildly, he then made his exit. We had just witnessed the most exciting and hardest working performer in show business!

James Brown had become such a popular performer and recording artist that he created most of his material and at the same time he was forging a change in the sound of soul. With his hits "Out Of Sight," "Papa's Got A Brand New Bag," and "I Got You" he took the music in directions totally different from other soul stars. Even though he also emphasized soulful singing, blaring horns, and a driving beat, he began to infuse touches of modern jazz and African rhythms into his music and called it "funky." (In Webster's New World Dictionary, funky is defined as "jazz having an earthy quality or style, derived from early blues or gospel music.") As the Beatles had in rock and roll, James Brown had gotten popular enough that he could afford to experiment. Like the Beatles, he began to insert messages into his music—such as the record, "Say It Loud, I'm Black And I'm Proud." These changes softened his music's edges.

There are other parallels between the Beatles' influence on rock and roll and James Brown's influence on R&B. In the 50's and early 60's cool whites were into both folk music and modern jazz, while cool blacks were into modern jazz. As the Beatles expanded popular rock and roll into the mainstream and included folk influences, more and more cool whites became fans; and as Brown mellowed his sound and included jazz influences, more and more cool blacks and whites became his fans. The Beatles, in their effort to broaden their audience, cheated good-time rock and roll. James Brown in his effort to broaden his base hurt original soulful R&B. Neither the Beatles nor Brown had a plan to take these changes as far as they went—things simply evolved.

A listing of prominent soul stars and some of their hit records are as follows:

James Brown- "I Got You," "Papa's Got A Brand New Bag," "It's A Man's Man's Man's World," "Cold Sweat (Part 1)," "I Got The Feelin'," "Say It Loud-I'm Black And I'm Proud"

Aretha Franklin- "I Never Loved A Man," "Respect," "Baby I Love You," "A Natural Woman," "Chain Of Fools," "Since You've Been Gone," "Think," "The House That Jack Built," "I Say A Little Prayer"

Otis Redding- "These Arms Of Mine," "Respect," "Satisfaction," "Try A Little Tenderness," "I've Been Loving You Too Long," "The Dock Of The Bay," "I Can't Turn You Loose," "Mr. Pitiful"

Sam and Dave- "Soul Man," "Hold On I'm Comin'," "I Thank You," "You Don't Know Like I Know," "When Something Is Wrong With My Baby," "You Don't Know What You Mean to Me"

Joe Tex- "Hold What You've Got," "Show Me," "Skinny Legs And All," " A Sweet Woman Like You"

Don Covay- "Mercy Mercy"

Eddie Floyd- "Knock On Wood," "Bring It On Home To Me"

Wilson Pickett- "In The Midnight Hour," "Don't Fight It," "If You Need Me," "Mustang Sally," "634-5789," "Land Of 1000 Dances," "Funky Broadway," "She's Lookin' Good"

Johnnie Taylor- "Who's Making Love"

William Bell- "You Don't Miss Your Water," "Private Number" (with Judy Clay)

Solomon Burke- "Just Out Of Reach," "Down In the Valley," "Got To Get You Off My Mind," "Cry To Me," "Tonight's The Night," "Hanging Up My Heart For You"

Arthur Conley- "Sweet Soul Music," "Funky, Street"

Etta James- "Tell Mama," "Security," "Pushover"

Carla Thomas- "Gee Whiz," "B.A.B.Y.," "Tramp" (with Otis Redding)

Percy Sledge-"When A Man Loves A Woman," "Cover Me," "Warm And Tender Love," "Take Time To Know Her"

Booker T. and the MG's- "Green Onions," "Time Is Tight," "Hang 'Em High," "Soul Limbo"

Rufus Thomas-"The Dog," "Walking The Dog," "Jump Back," "Do The Funky Chicken"

The other main bastion of black music during the 60's was the

Motown sound emanating out of Detroit, Michigan. Motown's records appealed to blacks and whites, like soul music, because of its upbeat, feel-good nature. During 1964-1969, only the Beatles had more number one records on the pop charts than did Motown's sensational trio, the Supremes. Taken collectively, the Motown labels—Soul, Gordy, Motown and Tamla were the most consistently successful of any record company during the decade. We service guys were immediately hooked on Motown.

And from the beginning, label founder Berry Gordy's vision of Motown was clear. Not only did he know very well what he wanted, he was non-compromising in his pursuits. He hired studio musicians, the Funk Brothers, for the exact sound he wanted. He used the back-up singers he wanted. Motown's songwriters wrote a steady stream of songs featuring compelling lyrics telling emotional, identifiable stories—plus the music was some of the catchiest in recording history. The most prolific and prominent of the songwriter-producer teams at Motown was made up of Edward Holland, Jr., Lamont Dozier and Brian Holland. Anyone recording in a major sound studio today would be nonplused to see the tiny square footage comprising the studio nicknamed the "Snakepit."

In his book, <u>Temptations</u>[18] with Patricia Romanowski, Otis Williams of the Temptations talks about those days, " . . . Generally, we could cut a track in three to four hours and wrap up a whole album inside a week. Even though today technology affords artists the chance to make perfect records, they still haven't come up with the machine that puts in that special electricity and energy of those live records."

Another distinction of the Motown operation was the strong conviction that the artists' images be perfectly honed, from wardrobe, make-up and hair-styling, to extensive choreography which was aptly dubbed Motown U. Berry Gordy demanded and received poise and professionalism from the entire Motown stable of artists. Nothing that came out of "Hitsville USA" was an accident.

The following is a sampling of Motown artists and some of their hits in the 60's:

Barrett Strong-"Money"
Mary Wells-"You Beat Me To The Punch," "The One Who Really Loves You," "My Guy," "Two Lovers"

The Contours- "Do You Love Me"
Marvin Gaye- "Stubborn Kind Of Fellow," "Pride And Joy," "How Sweet It Is," "I'll
    Be Doggone," "Ain't That Peculiar," "I Heard It Through The Grapevine"
Martha and the Vandellas- "Heat Wave," "Quicksand," "Dancing In The Street,"
    "Nowhere To Run," "I'm Ready For Love," "Jimmy Mack"
The Marvelettes- "Please Mr. Postman," "Playboy," "Beechwood 4-5789," "Don't
    Mess With Bill"
The Temptations- "The Way You Do The Things You Do," "My Girl," "Ain't Too
    Proud To Beg," "Beauty's Only Skin Deep," "I'm Losing You," "All I Need,"
    "You're My Everything," "I Wish It Would It Would Rain"
Stevie Wonder- "Fingertips," "Uptight," "Blowin' In The Wind," "A Place In The
    Sun," I Was Made To Love Her," "Shoo-Be-Doo-Be-Doo-Da-Day," "For Once In
    My Life," "My Cherie Amour,"
The Four Tops- "Baby I Need Your Loving," "I Can't Help Myself," "It's The Same
    Old Song," "Reach Out I'll Be There," "Standing In The Shadows Of Love,"
    "Bernadette," "Something About You"
The Supremes- "Where Did Our Love Go," "Baby Love," "Stop In The Name Of Love,"
    "Come See About Me," "Back In My Arms Again," "I Hear A   Symphony,"
    "My World Is Empty Without You," "Love Is Like An Itching In My Heart,"
    "You Can't Hurry Love," "You Keep Me Hanging On," "Love Is Here And Now
    You've Gone," "The Happening," "Reflections," "In And Out Of Love," "Love
    Child," "I'm Livin' In Shame," "Someday We'll Be Together"
Jimmy Ruffin- "What Becomes Of The Broken Hearted"
Brenda Holloway- "Every Little Bit Hurts"
The Miracles- "Shop Around," "You've Really Got A Hold On Me," "Mickey's
    Monkey, "Ooo, Baby, Baby," "The Tracks Of My Tears," "I Second That
    Emotion"
The Jackson 5- "I Want You Back"
Jr. Walker and the All Stars- "Shotgun," "What Does It Take," "I'm A Roadrunner"

In San Antonio, my black service friends like sergeants Johnston
Claire, George Norman and Landon Jackson seemed more in tune with
cool jazz music than with R&B. The jazz they liked and talked about was
progressive jazz, not the old-time New Orleans Dixieland style, of which
I was especially fond. I wondered if my friends were the exception, or
were blacks into jazz as a whole, more so than into R&B? Also I wondered if black support for R&B in general was beginning to waver and
even wane.

    As the 60's wore on there simply was not as much black music
being recorded. America's golden music was the only extremely popular
music type in history not to follow the traditional bell-shaped curve of

popularity and run its course. The music industry, in its rush to cash in on the British Invasion and the subsequent fallout, quit recording it in favor of recording rock music targeted to white teens.

Then, in 1968, an event occurred at the NATRA (National Association of Television and Radio Announcers) convention in Miami, Florida that had a further negative effect on blacks in the eyes of the recording industry. Nelson George, in <u>The Death Of Rhythm & Blues</u>[19], explains, "There was a lot of talk among people in the industry about 'pressure' being applied-black activists were strong-arming white record company owners for 'reparations for past exploitation' . . .

. . . At Miami, between August 14 and 18, white record men and black radio men were threatened, and some were beaten. Marshall Seahorn, Bobby Robinson's old New Orleans contact, was beaten. Phil Walden, Otis Redding's white manager, was threatened. So was Jerry Wexler . . . " This led to a wholesale defection of record labels and executives from black music—to rock music, Atlantic and Wexler being prime examples.

Original R&B declined, too. Black record buyers have historically turned their backs on black artists once they become too popular among whites. It has been viewed as selling out to whites, an "Uncle Tom" syndrome. In the 60's this became even more commonplace. Artist Muddy Waters learned the hard way. <u>Bluesland</u>[20], edited by Pete Welding and Toby Brown reveals, "By this time, however, Waters and other blues performers of his generation had been discovered and taken up by a new audience—young, white, and middle class—born of the folk music revival of the late fifties and swelled even further a few years later by the British blues boom. The audience was large, enthusiastic, and affluent, and it took to Waters in a big way.

. . . And while he was confused and hurt by the defection of black listeners, and couldn't understand their turning away from the blues, Waters was nothing if not pragmatic. If he couldn't play for blacks any longer, why then he'd play for whites, for anyone who'd listen . . . "

White fans of R&B like me were being left behind in the wake of these changes in black music itself. The British invasion began to gradually turn into a socially-driven protest music, and both the media and the record industry gobbled it up as though it were the only "happening" music on the scene. We fans of America's golden music felt that we were being blitzed from both sides, and rapidly becoming fans without a country.

Television had already gained tremendous power and influence by the time the Beatles made their way into our living rooms. The barrage of news about the near-hysteria of hordes of screaming girls who followed them everywhere helped increase ratings and sponsorship as TV news became more profit-driven and less news-driven. And with the constant media attention, the Beatles began to take themselves seriously.

The media reported stories which dug deeper and deeper into their private lives. The Beatles later came under the influence of the "wisdom" of the Maharajah Mahareshi Yogi. Their robes, lengthening hair and beards greatly added to their mystique, and the facade of youthful innocence was becoming a distant memory. I watched all this coverage and attention on the nightly news in San Antonio and other places with disbelief because information about them, and its influence over their fans, was virtually spontaneous.

John Lennon was particularly witty and sharp, even acid-tongued at times. He was a reporter's dream interview and a guarantee of good copy; thus, the Beatles were a guarantee of good copy. The Beatles were seeking to have it both ways. They were still anti-establishment in appearance and deed—particularly John. For teenagers this overshadowed the almost forgotten, slight irritant of parents liking their music. Nothing could have better cemented this status than a comment made by Lennon about the Beatles being more popular than Jesus Christ. It created quite a stir—and many teens ate it up. Lennon's style irreverently poked fun at society's views. So with John and the Beatles, teen America had not only a group who served as their pied pipers, but a perfect, very vocal spokesperson. During the early stages I observed it all and found John and his antics harmlessly amusing.

The media had begun to align baby boomers with British influenced rock and roll—"rock." Not the innocent, fun-filled rock and roll of the early Beatles, but an anti-establishment message-filled music. After the successes of "Yesterday" and Michelle," rock and roll incorporated folk music under its umbrella and this branch was called folk rock. Folk singer and songwriter Bob Dylan's open acceptance and performing of rock and roll helped speed up the process. Folk purists were at first aghast at Dylan's "selling out," but eventually simply followed his lead and became folk rock junkies. Some of the artists who fell into this category and their songs were:

Bob Dylan- "Like A Rolling Stone," "Positively 4th Street," "Rainy Day Women,"
    "Lay Lady Lay"
The Byrds- "Mr. Tambourine Man," "Turn, Turn, Turn"
The Mamas and Papas- "California Dreamin'," "Monday, Monday," "I Saw Her Again,"
    "Words Of Love," "Dedicated To The One I Love," "Creque Alley"
Peter, Paul, and Mary- "I Dig Rock and Roll Music," "Leaving On A Jet Plane"
Donovan- "Sunshine Superman," "Mellow Yellow," "Hurdy Gurdy Man," "Atlantis"
Barry McGuire- "Eve Of Destruction"
Lovin' Spoonful- "Do You Believe In Magic," "You Didn't Have To Be So Nice,"
    "Daydream," "Did You Ever Have To Make Up Your Mind?," "Summer In The
    City," "Rain On The Roof," "Nashville Cats"
The Grass Roots- "Let's Live For Today," "Midnight Confessions"
Crispian St. Peters- "The Pied Piper"
Judy Collins- "Both Sides Now"
The Doors- "Light My Fire," "Hello, I Love You," "Touch Me," "People Are Strange"
Simon & Garfunkel- "The Sounds Of Silence," "Homeward Bound," "I Am A Rock,"
    "Mrs. Robinson," "The Boxer"
Strawberry Alarm Clock- "Incense And Peppermint"

Until the 60's, illegal drugs had been commonly viewed as something used only by street people, jazz musicians and the beatnik folk music crowd. The huge amount of publicity generated about the Fab Four's experimentation with illegal drugs was fast contributing to the popular acceptance of illegal drug use. And fans were as influenced by their lifestyles as by their music and many budding musicians were spawned from the Beatles' influence. For those who developed musical careers, part of the expected, if not requisite behavior included illegal drug use. This acceptance continued to broaden its effect, filtering down further and further into the mores of youth. Maybe I was blind, but I knew no service or college friends who used drugs. Some possibly did, but if so, I didn't know.

By an odd set of circumstances, there was also a growing division within the rock and roll community with regards to drug use. Alcohol, not illegal drugs, was used—if it all—by early American rock and rollers. This lack of illegal drug use contributed to their demise, because they were no longer perceived to be "with it" any more. It was no longer "in" to be nice and humble and neatly dressed. I have long admired the original rock and rollers—there has always been a classy dignity about most of them. But now they were out of the loop, and no longer the right kind of outrageous cool.

Just how "cool" the drug scene had become is illustrated by Mary Wilson of the Supremes in **Dreamgirl** [21] concerning the Supremes' visit with the Beatles while appearing on an Ed Sullivan show: "We entered the Beatles' suite, perfectly poised . . . the room reeked of marijuana smoke, but we kept on smiling through our introductions. It was difficult to be gracious and friendly in the face of what we could only see as the coolest reception we'd ever received. We felt that we had interrupted something . . . John Lennon just sat in a corner and stared.

. . .Years later, I was visiting George Harrison at his home in England. Recalling that first meeting, he said, 'We expected soulful, hip girls. We couldn't believe that three black girls from Detroit could be so square.'"

More and more "in" rock musicians began openly using drugs, and drug use spread into other areas of entertainment and into society in general. Celebrities in television, theater, movies, and sports were increasingly jailed for drug offenses. Yet, while I was repulsed by them and thought less of them for doing it, the rock community seemed to embrace them with open arms, and even to consider them as "heroes in arms" who were fighting the establishment. The "acceptance by use" message was being effectively passed down to young people.

Michelle Phillips in **California Dreamin'** [22] relates how the Mamas and Papas gained a new appreciation of what the Beatles' music was all about: "The LSD 25, the acid, was working wonders . . . And we heard, we heard the Beatles for the first time . . . In that moment we knew that we, this group of people . . . were going to make a transition in our music. We had to. I was just amazed that this new sound had been going on for some time because either I had not heard the Beatles, or, if I had heard them, I had not appreciated what or where they were at. Now I did, and so did the others, John, Denny, Cass. All." To Michelle and the others it clearly took the acid trip to really tune into the Beatles.

It is apparent that the Beatles' music was only part of what propelled them to the top. They were and are more symbol than substance.

They are still referred to as contemporaries even though it has been more than two decades since they have done anything together. At the same time a group like the Spinners, who had their biggest hits and success after the Beatles disbanded, are considered to be an oldies act, though still performing together. The Beatles helped define a style that has stayed with us even today.

An article by Drew Jubera in the June 18, 1992 edition of the Atlanta **Constitution**[23] gives Paul McCartney's perspective on the Beatles' influence: "We had the power to be like Hitler then, and it's lucky that we turned out as we did. The Beatles have largely been a force for the good. In fact, I think we were great, one of the best things to come out of the 20th century."

True, their power was much like Hitler's, but the rest of McCartney's view is well off the mark! They led the way to an acceptable intertwining of rock music with illegal drugs which, I believe, has had a direct link with today's out-of-control drug scene and its subsequent off-shoots. The Beatles' and their peers' irreverent, arrogant attitudes and life-styles, and their flaunting of open sex have been glamorized by the media and readily embraced by successive generations of impressionable and receptive young people who upon reaching adulthood still act like irresponsible teenagers. When their influence is analyzed in its totality, the Beatles phenomenon may have been one of the most dangerous things to come out of the 2Oth Century!

18 Otis Williams with Patricia Romanowski, *Temptations* (New York, 1988). p. 91.
19 George, pp. 114-115.
20 Pete Welding and Toby Brown, *Bluesland* (New York, 1991). p. 154.
21 Mary Wilson, *Dreamgirl* (New York, 1986). p. 214.
22 Phillips, p. 54.
23 Drew Jubera, "Can It Be? Paul Turns 50," Atlanta *Constitution*, June 18, 1992, p. F4.

CHAPTER 12

RAMBLIN' MAN

In the spring semester of 1966 I was "Back To School Again" (a 50's hit by Timmie "Oh Yeah" Rogers) having completed my stint in the Air Force. This time I arrived with a new positive attitude, a newly-found ability to study properly, and a used 1961 white Chevrolet. Guys' hair was much longer than when I left in 1962, and students were dressing somewhat more sloppily and possessed a much looser attitude. Surprisingly, even some instructors appeared more lackadaisical. I wondered if it was because I was more mature and less intimidated, but decided that there were unquestionable differences. But for the first time in my life I was attacking the college scene with a definite goal in mind. After one semester of dorm life, I shared a dumpy, non-air-conditioned apartment with another service veteran, Randy Chambers, in what is arguably the hottest city in the U.S.-Columbia, S.C. Yet, as much as I disliked the heat, it sure did beat dormitory life.

Still, the music of choice was R&B. The rock scene was alive in Columbia, but it was confined to small pockets of students. Rock was much slower in gaining popularity on Southeastern campuses. There was a good bit of R&B played on popular radio stations, WCOS-AM and WNOK-AM. WCOS's DJ Woody Wyndham had a real love for R&B, and played a good dose of it. He once had so many requests for "Stubborn Kind Of Fellow", an "oldie" by Marvin Gaye, that it went again to number one on WCOS's popular music chart. (Woody has continued his career to this day as one of Columbia's most popular DJ's.)

In San Antonio, the juke boxes had been filled with rock music, so it was refreshing to find that almost all of the juke boxes in Columbia night spots still primarily featured R&B. Don's, a club we frequented located in the Five Points area near the campus, had a juke box which contained songs such as "Tracks Of My Tears" by Smokey Robinson and the Miracles, "Since I Lost My Baby" by the Temptations, "What Becomes Of The Broken Hearted" by Jimmy Ruffin, and songs by the Drifters, Otis Redding, the Four Tops, James Brown, Mitch Ryder and the Detroit Wheels, Joe Tex, Sam and Dave, Wilson Pickett, and Barbara Lewis. Folk music, the rage when I left in 1962, was nowhere to be found.

Several USC students from Greenwood, S.C. had formed a good-time rock and roll/R&B group called the Swinging Medallions. They hit the national charts with a song called "Double Shot (Of My Baby's Love)." To this day, the Swinging Medallions still perform throughout the Southeast, and the party anthem "Double Shot" is a must at every performance.

Shortly before graduation, a friend, Allan Strait, and I went to see James Brown at Columbia's Township Auditorium. It was the usual stellar James Brown show, but "Soul Brother Number One" had added a new element. He used flashing strobe lights during his performance, which enhanced the swiftness of his movements. It was probably an attempt to broaden his appeal to whites who at that time were mesmerized by light effects and psychedelia.

On occasion, several of us would get together, buy a couple of six-packs of beer, and listen to a wonderfully, strange radio voice emanating from radio station, XTRF-AM, that broadcast from Ciudad Acuña, Mexico. The voice belonged to a man who howled like a wolf, and went by the handle of "The Wolf Man." It was our first experience with the cult hero, Wolfman Jack. He played some great R&B music, and we were hooked on his radio show. He later moved to Tijuana, Mexico, and radio station XTRA, where he became a superstar to Southern California listeners. The Wolfman was the last original and refreshing DJ. He has had a real love for America's rock and roll and has kept it alive through radio, TV and promotion of live performances featuring its artists. Sadly, the AM radio "personality" rock and roll DJ's were about to become extinct. Wolfman Jack was the last of a breed.

It was with a satisfied and excited feeling that I hugged my parents, kissed my girlfriend Pat goodbye, got in my car and exited Columbia with my degree and the rest of my life before me. Finally getting out of dreaded school once and for all, I let out a long, fading wolf howl—the unforgettable signoff of Wolfman Jack.

Upon graduation, I was offered a position as Trade Examiner with one of Atlanta's and the world's best known companies, The Coca-Cola Company. It was a suitcase job, and I traveled throughout the United States. I never really lived in Atlanta then, even though that had been my intention.

In October, 1967 my first assignment took me to Providence, Rhode Island for training. Cold weather was beginning to settle in, and I found it to be starkly beautiful. From the textile mill towns of Fall River and Worcester, Massachusetts, to the ornate mansions that dotted the Newport, Rhode Island area, the New Englanders could not have been more delightful.

Nevertheless, I was slapped across the face by the total dominance of rock music on area radio stations. I could not believe my eyes as I spied a poster on a wall in the slums of downtown Providence. It was advertising the appearance of Aaron Neville at a local dive. Less than a year earlier, Aaron had had a number two hit on the national music charts! It was an R&B, New Orleans style song called "Tell It Like It Is." Chillingly, I felt as if I had been relocated to a music "Siberia."

One place I heard some great music, however, was in Yarmouth, Maine, when I was invited to visit one of my old Air Force roommates, Dave Seabury. Riding the bus to Maine, the area was just as I had pictured. There was snow blanketing the ground, but the cozy homes in the Yarmouth area cast a friendly glow. The shoreline was breathtakingly beautiful. It was a pleasure to see Dave again, and to meet his family. We had a great time listening to music and reminiscing, while we feasted on lobster. Duane Eddy, Gene Pitney, and the Righteous Brothers were Dave's particular favorites and Dave, his girlfriend and I stayed up until late night listening to music by firelight.

My trainer, Joe Dillard, and I spent the next month operating out of a hotel in Manhattan. I was able to tune into some good R&B on the radio. "I Heard It Through The Grapevine" by Gladys Knight and the Pips had just reached number one on the New York City music charts. Sadly, it was during my stay that the great Otis Redding met his tragic death, which had a numbing effect on me. A caller to a New York radio station wanted to know why Otis' death didn't receive more prominent attention and she only confirmed what I was feeling at the time.

April 4, 1968 found me in Knoxville, Tennessee typing up forms with the TV going in my motel room. I was jerked to attention by a bulletin saying that Dr. Martin Luther King, Jr. had just been shot in Memphis. After it was announced that he was dead, R&B played a peacekeeping role. James Brown was called on in both Boston and Washington to help calm aroused crowds. His Boston performance was even televised live by a public TV station and helped keep many potential trouble-makers off the streets. I felt a certain amount of pride for Brown's efforts, as well as sadness and apprehension as to what would happen in society as a result of King's death.

After spending weeks slamming suitcases, I arrived in one of my favorite places, Albuquerque, New Mexico, in late April of 1968. I fell in love with the area. The days were warm and the nights pleasantly cool. One could see for miles and miles, with Sandia Peak nearby, and Mount Taylor in the distance. The people were exceedingly friendly, and diverse groups like whites, blacks, Hispanics, and Native Americans, co-existed in real harmony. There were a couple of clubs that featured R&B type singers, Charlie Brown and Duke Washington, and I honed in on them in a hurry. I made several friends, including Charlie and Duke, and still look upon the easy, comfortable Albuquerque lifestyle with fondness.

After leaving Albuquerque, it was on to scenic and unique places like Santa Fe and Los Alamos, New Mexico, Durango, Colorado, and Rock Springs, Wyoming. Next I headed to California for a lengthy stay with examiner Jack Lang in the Oakland-San Francisco Bay area. While enroute I heard the news that another of my favorite performers had passed away—Little Willie John. He died in Washington State Prison in Walla Walla, Washington. He had been incarcerated for killing a man in a brawl. Gone was yet another artist I would never see or hear in person again. Wistfully, I could hear his hits, "Fever," "Talk to Me, Talk To Me," "Let Them Talk," and "Sleep" playing over and over in my head. The music I loved was slipping further and further out of reach.

And listening to the news while driving to California, I noticed that the media centered their broadcasts on the "hippies" and the "love generation." I recalled my first visit to the Bay area a year earlier where the hippies lived in the Haight-Ashbury district of San Francisco. Richard

Brassell and I had attended a 49ers-Atlanta Falcons football game at Kezar Stadium, near Haight-Ashbury. We had felt eerily uneasy as we walked through hordes of dirty, unkempt, spaced-out "flower children" that chilly, foggy afternoon.

I was really slapped across the face by the unfolding hippie, anti-establishment, anti-war, drug-related rock music way of life when I finally arrived in Oakland. It was everywhere in northern California! The movement had a certain look—dirty, faded jeans, tie-dyed t-shirts, stringy long hair, bare feet, love beads and straggly beards—the absolute opposite of the neat, buttoned-down norm of the day. They claimed to be non-conformists, yet they looked very much alike.

Swelling numbers of young Californians began to dress like hippies and demonstrated for social causes. There were reports of fire-bombings, burnings of buildings and such. The media's tone seemed more than sympathetic to their causes and television in particular became obsessed with daily reports—these young protesters became media "darlings." The media began casting civil rights actions by inner city blacks in a more disparaging light after young whites shifted most of their energies from civil rights to the anti-Vietnam war movement (after all, it more directly affected them.)

The "call to arms" was sex, drugs and rock and roll! What was now called rock music had become almost totally Caucasian, thoroughly British-influenced, and completely stripped of its original American sound. Increasingly, rockers became avowed, even proud drug users, as did their followers and fans. Rock now also had its own magazine which gave it greater authenticity and critical acceptance. <u>Heroes & Villains</u>[24] author Steven Gaines reveals, " . . . A new magazine published in San Francisco, '<u>Rolling Stone</u>' (whose first issue included a free roach clip), coalesced the idea that rock musicians were modern-day minstrels, responsible for delivering socially relevant messages. They wrote anti-establishment, antiwar, pro-love songs, and songs that spoke of the magic of drugs." The media swallowed it up and spit it out for the public, and I couldn't believe the immediate acceptance and credibility that <u>Rolling Stone</u> received, and in turn gave to the rock counterculture movement, warts and all.

Jack and I had calls near the Telegraph Avenue area at the University of California, so we stopped for a beer at one of the hang-outs after finishing work for the day. There was <u>nothing</u> but ear-piercing hard rock and folk rock on the juke box. Everyone appeared to be involved in very deep, serious conversations amid the pungent odor of marijuana smoke. We both remarked that we were the only people who seemed to be enjoying ourselves. We thought that a bar was a place to have a good time and relax, but evidently not on Telegraph Avenue!

With anticipation, I drove across the bay to San Francisco to date an old friend, Marilyn, who was a Delta Airlines stewardess. She seemed pleased to see me and, as we talked over dinner, I related my experience on Telegraph Avenue, and how everybody seemed so extremely serious and intense. She looked at me grimly and crisply stated that with the war and such, there was absolutely nothing to smile about. Any attempt to inject humor was met with a steel eye and the remainder of the evening went downhill quickly.

Michelle Phillips described Marilyn's attitude in <u>California Dreamin'</u>[25]: "We were somehow all one, and, as the Beatles said, life flowed on within us and without us. We were, despite our individual snobberies, so tolerant as long as people were **cool!**"

Jack suggested that we take a week-end trip to Las Vegas. I agreed and off we went. As we drove into Vegas, Jack knew every landmark. But what really surprised me was that the casino dealers all knew Jack by name. The man obviously had a side that I knew nothing about, and we had a ball that week-end! We saw Fats Domino and Ella Fitzgerald and got their autographs. We went to see comedian Don Rickles, but the mood was too strained for comedy, as Robert Kennedy had been assassinated a few days earlier.

With the exception of Fats Domino, big name R&B and even rock performers were almost non-existent on the Las Vegas strip. In 1968 it was a glitzy gambling town that appealed primarily to middle-aged and older, more affluent types. Still, Fats seemed to have moved very comfortably in the Las Vegas scene, and his act was very well supported by the high rollers. But Dick Clark changed that shortly thereafter and presented the first of his oldies rock and roll shows at one of the casinos.

What beautiful country spread before me as I made my way to Oregon and calls in Klamath Falls, Medford, Ashland, Roseburg, Corvallis, Eugene, and Salem. The aroma of wood smoke from numerous timber processing plants permeated the entire region, and today that

Daddy & Betty
First date
1948

Seven year old
Harry reading
a comic book
at the piano
1949

Housekeeper Irene
(at right) and friends
ready to go to
Atlantic Beach
1957

The original Inkspots--
Bill Kenny, Hoppy Jones, Deek Watson, Charlie Fuqua--
1936 to 1944
(Courtesy Millie Della Lilley)

"Shake, Rattle & Roll"--
Big Joe Turner- 1985
(Courtesy Mrs. Joe Turner)

Hugh "Baby" Jarrett,
member of Jordanaires
(Elvis' back-up group),
also DJ on WLAC,
Nashville-- 1990.
(Courtesy Hugh Jarrett)

Young Jessie--
"Mary Lou"
--1992.
(Courtesy Obie Jessie)

Legendary shagger
Harry Driver at home
in Dunn, N. C. with
his wife Dottie-- 1992.
(Courtesy Harry Driver)

Joey Dee and the Starliters--
Joey Dee, Larry Vernieri, David Brigati
at the George M. Cohan monument in New York-- 1962.
(Courtesy Joey Dee)

The Impressions celebrate
Curtis Mayfield's birthday--
Sam Gooden, Curtis, Fred Cash
mid-1960's (Courtesy Curtis Mayfield)

The Tams--
Robert Smith, Joe Jones, Charles Pope, Horace Key,
Joe Pope (on stool)-- 1980's.
(Courtesy Robert Smith)

Wolfman Jack
in the studio
--1990's
(Courtesy Dell Long)

Archie Bell and
Harry in studio
at WRDX-FM,
Salisbury, N. C.
--1988
(Courtesy
Archie Bell)

The Clovers--
John Bowie, Johnny Mason, founder Harold Lucas,
Steve Charles-- 1980's.
(Courtesy Mike Evans and Steve Charles)

The Legendary
Orioles--
Diz Russell,
Reese Palmer,
Gerald
Holeman,
Skip Mahoney,
Eddie Jones
at the National
Arboretum,
Washington,
D.C. -- 1982
(Courtesy
Millie Russell)

Rock and Roll Hall of Famer Hank Ballard (right) with singer Billy Scott
at Lake Lure Inn -- 1986 (Courtesy John Mojjis).

The Del -Vikings--
Dave Lerchey, Norman Wright, John Byas, Kripp Johnson (seated)
--1980's (Courtesy Millie Della Lilley)

The Flamingos in
performance at
Lake Lure Inn--
Jake Carey,
Archie
Satterfield,
Bennie Cherry,
Zeke Carey--
1988 (Courtesy
John Mojjis)

"Dirty Dancing Revue,"
dancers Jan Smith and
Jeffrey White at Lake
Lure, N. C. -- 1988
(Courtesy John Mojjis)

Maurice Williams receiving
a platinum album from the
movie's writer Eleanor
Bergstein, for his hit song
"Stay," which was on the
Dirty Dancing soundtrack
album. Also pictured John
Mojjis, owner Lake Lure
Inn, 1988
(Courtesy John Mojjis)

Actor Patrick Swayze
dancing at Lake Lure
Inn during filming of
Dirty Dancing-- 1986
(Courtesy John Mojjis)

Legendary WLAC
DJ John R.
(John Richbourg)
at the mike-- 1970's
(Courtesy Dell
Long)

Nine time national shag
dance champions
Charlie Womble and
Jackie McGee in action--
1986 (Courtesy Jackie
McGee)

Fats Domino and fan with Harry backstage
at the Fox Theatre in Atlanta-- 1986

Dee Clark and
Carla Thomas
with Harry at
T'Bird's in
Atlanta-- 1990
(Courtesy
Harold
Anderson)

Irene Roberts,
proprietor of
Lone Oak
Motel, Toccoa,
Ga. where Dee
Clark lived in
the last years
of his life--
1993

Before the Saints-Falcons game, Clarence "Frogman" Henry (holding Rush Limbaugh's book which features a story about "Frogman") and Harry revive their football rivalry-- 1993.

Marv Johnson and Harry talk in Atlanta-- 1993
(Courtesy Susan Mather)

Bill Pinkney of the Drifters, Mike Campbell (son of S.C. Governor Carroll Campbell) and Harry at reception for Bill at the Governor's Mansion-- 1993.

Bill Pinkney and the Original Drifters--
Richard Knight, Russell Henry, Chuck Cockerham, Bill Pinkney (bottom)-- 1993.
(Courtesy Bill Pinkney)

Ray Peterson performing at the Drifters' 40th anniversary concert in Sumter, S.C.-- 1993.
(Courtesy Ray Peterson)

Singer Arthur Epps (former singer with Bill Pinkney and the Original Drifters) at the old Capricorn Recording Studio (now Phoenix Sound Studio) in Macon, Ga.-- 1993 (Courtesy Arthur Epps)

Singer George Smith, former Ink Spot and vocalist with Lionel Hampton-- 1993.

Doris Jackson and her Shirelles (Fanita James, Gloria Jones) with Harry, wife Jean, promoter Ron Simpson at Roswell Mill in Atlanta-- 1993. (Courtesy Talmadge and Eugene Stuckey)

smell brings back pleasant memories.

Finally, I settled in Portland, Oregon for a month. James Brown and his orchestra came to the local coliseum shortly after my arrival. Naturally, I attended, along with an enthusiastic audience of about 8,000 and it was the usual energetic show, with possibly even better musicians than before. The staff writer in the next day's Portland <u>Oregonian</u> gave the show and the band rave reviews. I felt a little touch of home that evening, because out west, there simply wasn't much R&B played on the radio. Except . . .

In Portland, I discovered my first all-oldies station on the car radio as I drove throughout the area. The station offered a great mix of oldies, including a good bit of R&B. It blew me away to think that I first heard this new and unique concept in a distant suburb of Portland, Oregon, because for years I had felt it could work well in the South. However, it was a couple of years before I heard an oldies format back home.

That summer, the media continued massive coverage of anti-war demonstrations and the counterculture movement. The anti-war movement was gaining a real head of steam, and it came together at the Democratic National Convention in Chicago. Live footage of the ongoing disturbances, often fraught with law enforcement brutality, was aired nightly. Though appalled at the violence, I was equally disturbed by the obvious lack of respect for authority by young demonstrators. There were those fighting serious battles within their own consciences; but there were many who were simply quintessential "rebels without a cause" (like Marlon Brando's and James Dean's characters had been) or rebels for other reasons.

A young boy confessed to me that he was happy he failed his Army physical because he didn't want to go into the service and face its discipline. When I asked him how many of his friends were true pacifists, he replied, "I don't know any pacifists, all my friends feel like me. They just don't want to go in the service, and all that hippie, anti-war stuff has just made it easier to get by with it."

The media portrayed the movement as espousing peace and love: "Make love, not war." (Ironically, not "Be loving, don't make war.") It was as though the hedonistic "<u>Playboy</u> philosophy" was replacing the "wisdom of the ages." When demonstrators threw profanities around and chanted "kill the pigs"—a reference to police—I wondered about their true motives. Yet politicians, advertisers, marketers and the entertainment industry had also readily embraced this vocal minority as though they represented the vast majority of young people. I couldn't believe it, as I knew very few who were adopting that lifestyle.

Alliances make strange bedfellows—the key ally was added to the mix that would send things spinning out of control! The media had convinced parents that they had raised a "wise generation" of caring youngsters and that their excesses were no more than "kids being kids." So even if they disagreed with their kids' dress, blatant sexual proclivities, use of drugs and screeching rock music, increasingly, mainstream parents tacitly approved of the hippie movement. Counterculture members were now literally given blank checks to do whatever they wanted with little or no accountability for their actions!

Michelle Phillips[26] explains the "specialness" of her generation in her book and admits that they made a mistake by believing " . . . that original sin had fled the Love Generation."

24 Steven Gaines, *Heroes & Villains* (New York, 1986), p. 154.
25 Phillips, p. 144.
26 Ibid., p. 142.

CHAPTER 13

THE MUSICAL DOLDRUMS

Rock and roll had split into two separate and distinct categories by the late 60's: original American, black-based, danceable rock and roll—America's golden music, an honest and fun-filled music; the other was white-based, British-influenced, primarily for listening, now called rock music. It was drug-oriented, serious, and message-filled with a particular emphasis against the Vietnam war. And the division was being formed along sociological lines. America's golden music was the music of the young establishment while rock was the music of the counterculture. Sadly, the recording industry and marketers almost totally embraced rock music as the music for the prized baby boom market—and almost equally ignored America's golden music, despite the love for it by millions of fans like me.

In 1969 I put my love of music on hold as I fulfilled my family's goals for me. Since I was a boy, it had been drummed into me that the only way "to make it" in life was to get a college degree, go to work for a large corporation, and get married. So I put my traveling days behind me and became a management trainee in the textile industry in Spartanburg, S.C. Getting married was supposed to make life complete as Mary Ann Harmon and I said our wedding vows. But there was something missing and I didn't know what—and so the hardest years for me to endure in my entire life were those from 1969 to 1976.

Sunday, July 20, 1969 stood out as a day when a page in history turned for the world, but especially for me. The radio newscast on our way home from church carried only three news items—the Apollo Moon landing, Mary Jo Kopechne's death in Senator Ted Kennedy's car at Chappaquiddick, and the death of singer Roy Hamilton. The first two were landmark news stories, while the third was nothing but a news blip to most. But to me, the death of the "Golden Voice" was a stunning blow. He was only 40 years old, and one of the greatest singers who ever lived. God how I loved Roy's singing of "Unchained Melody," "You'll Never Walk Alone," "Don't Let Go," and "You Can Have Her." I had missed his performance in Greenville only a couple of months before—and damnit, I had never seen him in person . . . and never would. Roy's death paralleled for me the dying nature of America's golden music from the viewpoint of the media and recording industry—and at the same time the moon landing seemed to be the last gasp of pure American pride and Chappaquiddick foretold the societal sleeze that was just around the corner.

Later that summer the Sharon Tate murders shook the country, and so did the news of the darker, more violent side to the hippie movement as an ultimate evil sprang from hippie communes—Charles Manson and his murderous band of followers who committed those murders. An admitted influence for the slaughtering rampage in Southern California, as chronicled in Vincent Bugliosi's book <u>Helter Skelter</u> about the Manson gang, was the Beatles' song "Helter Skelter" from their "White Album", and Manson's interpretation of its call for a race war.

One of Charles Manson's forays into the radically oriented echelons of rock involved Dennis Wilson of the Beach Boys. The Beach Boys had begun to adopt many of the airs and habits of British influenced rock stars, having abandoned their clean cut image. Steven Gaines in his book <u>Heroes</u> <u>&</u> <u>Villains</u>[27], writes,. . . Confused, depressed about his impending divorce, and very stoned, Dennis was the perfect prey for Charlie. . . Dennis was sufficiently impressed by Charlie and his girls to ask them to move in with him . . "

Charles Manson even wrote a song for the Beach Boys. Gaines explains[28], " . . . the song was released by Capitol Records on the B side of the first single from the soon-to-be-released '20/20' album, backing 'Bluebirds over the Mountain.' The single never got past number 61, but the Beach Boys had put Charles Manson on the charts." Why did this association with one of the most heinous psychopaths in history not even make a small dent in the Beach Boys' reputation nor their career? Was it covered up at the time, or was it just another case of outrageous behavior being expected and accepted by a curiously skewed rebellious fan mentality? The Beach Boys by that time no longer sounded the same to me.

And as these difficult and unsettling years passed, Mary Ann and I had three children and became active in the Presbyterian church. We enrolled our kids in organized sports and piano lessons, and found ourselves on the fast track of shuttling them to and from these pursuits. I loved my children, but subrogating my life to them was something else again. And this was the American dream? There had to be more to life than the rut we were in.

Settling into the "proper lifestyle" had put my involvement in music and my dreams on the backburner, but not my mind. The ongoing changes in the music industry and radio were obvious and disturbing. The age of hype, gimmickry, and yet, at the same time, blandness was upon us. It was now creeping into all levels of entertainment.

The recording industry was becoming extremely modernized. Technical quality, to the point of excess, was the key component, which allowed the recordings of inferior talents to be turned into near perfect products. No longer were the singers and musicians in the studio together, capturing each other's energy and excitement. Individual tracks were now recorded on different days, in different studios, in different cities, sometimes even in different countries—then put together by a master engineer, who could eliminate all flaws. The day of the electronic wizard engineers as the real industry stars was now a reality and the decrease in the number of records I was buying reflected my feelings. I bought a few Motown recordings and occasional records by favorite artists like Gladys Knight and the Pips and a budding star named Al Green, but not much else that was new.

This sterilization process was so obvious to me, but I felt that nobody else realized what was happening or cared. However, American artists from the original days of rock and roll (I found out later) noticed. Singer Connie Francis in her book, <u>Who's Sorry Now</u>[29] explains her feelings about the changes: "What's almost as sad is the fact that the fun's all gone-the spontaneity, the challenge, the surge of excitement you experience when you know you've come up with a great new sound, a smash hit right on the spot. You just can't beat that feeling when you leave a session knowing that with a little bit of luck, you've got it made. Shame on all guilty persons for hurting such a great industry." [30]

"Whenever someone says to me: 'That's not the way it's done anymore,' my first question to them is: 'Not done by whom? And why not? I was not an iconoclast—because sometimes there was a good reason, but more often, there was not."

The growing numbers of rock music fans in the Carolinas joined a nationwide movement to "underground radio." Up to this time, AM had been the dominant radio band. The FM radio band had contained fewer licensed frequencies, and the formats had been largely classical, semi-classical, Broadway show tunes, Mantovani strings—elevator music. Aside from occasional sports programming, or AM programs simulcast on their frequencies, commercials and talk were held to a minimum. Many radio receivers didn't even receive FM signals. So FM was the exception, the oddity—"underground radio." FM radio was considered illicit by the radio establishment, which suited its counterculture listeners just fine.

The FM band had a number of distinct advantages over the AM band, mainly clarity of signal, and lack of electrical interference. Stereo—two channel recording—had been on the market for about a decade, but only the FM band could broadcast in stereo. Young rockers reveled in recordings using electronic guitar and keyboard gimmicks. These sounds were greatly enhanced and distinguished by stereo separation, so underground radio immediately established its place in rock music, attracting young fans in hordes.

Throughout the 70's, both the number of FM stations and listener-ship grew by leaps and bounds. WFBC-FM in Greenville began to take listeners away from both WORD-AM in Spartanburg and WQOK-AM in Greenville, and there were similar occurrences all over the U.S. With the wider range of FM signals, regional radio was born, and AM radio lost much of its strength. FM stations had gained both a larger reach and a larger revenue base, which also increased their influence on the music industry from a music chart reporting standpoint. FM had finally supplanted AM radio in dominance by the end of the decade.

FM radio developed the "12 in a row" format—twelve records played back to back without interruption, followed by a cluster of commercials, while AM radio stayed with its traditional news at the top of the hour, two or three records, followed by announcer patter, commercials, then two or three more records, and so on.

94

With the rise in FM radio, it became too risky to leave much to the DJ's discretion, as had been the case with AM. Program directors became programming gods. Playlists were "scientifically" determined by demographic formulas, record rotation was mathematically figured, and DJ's maintained precious little, if any, autonomy and personal judgment. Talk became a dirty word. Other than the obligatory hip and flippant morning drive personalities, DJ's became nothing more than mechanical platter spinners, with any talk scripted, read from cue cards at specific parts of the hour.

As I travelled around the country during that time, I noticed that FM radio formats had become very much alike, and there have been very few changes since. So-called "expert" consultants began positioning themselves as "saviors," and stations nationwide bought their services. In **Radio Waves**[21], Los Angeles DJ Jim Ladd describes their influence: "And therein lay the genius of the radio consultant, a man who looked out onto the broad landscape of rock radio's beautiful and chaotic diversity, and saw the future: generic radio: safe, uniform, nonthreatening; an entire nation of independent voices, melded into a monotone of sameness, and all under the direction of the radio consultant and his formula."

FM-dominated radio had put the once vibrant radio business into the doldrums, and had left it largely without personality or character. Even different music formats—country, rock, oldies, album-oriented rock, classic rock, urban contemporary-all sounded alike except for the music. And so "robotic" radio was born during the 70's and since then true creativity has almost ceased to exist.

It became next to impossible for unknown recording artists, no matter how talented, to get airplay on FM stations. They played only what was safe, what was proven—which amounted to playing only the records that large record companies promoted. Payola lived on, just on a more sophisticated level. Since then the formulaic FM radio-recording industry alliance has been like a massive, monotonous monopoly, with the big guys getting bigger and richer, and the small guys never getting a chance. Few have been willing to break out of this groove, and sadly, mediocrity has abounded. An acquaintance who owned both an AM and FM station in the Carolinas asked me one day, "Do you know what FM really stands for?" "No, what?" "Feeble minded—because to listen to FM, one surely doesn't have to think."

Not only did the counterculture spawn a radical change in radio, it did in fashion as well. Mature men who had worn their hair neatly trimmed all their lives began letting it grow long and dropped their sideburns the length of their cheeks. Women began to take on the look of the "love child." Jeans became quite the rage—not neat new jeans, but jeans with holes, patches, pre-washed, bleached—the sloppier the better. And, of course, there were bell-bottom trousers, hip-huggers and the braless look. This whole movement went against my upbringing and beliefs, and I was dumbfounded as I watched people become influenced by this lifestyle.

Glitz and glamour was now fast becoming a driving force in society and even my favorite sport was being affected. I had always liked CBS's and NBC's "the game's the thing" approach to televising pro football. Being a super fan, I eagerly awaited NFL Monday Night Football's start in 1970. ABC-TV proceeded to make Frank Gifford (his predecessor Keith Jackson) and his partners, Howard Cosell and Don Meredith, more important than the game itself. In <u>Monday Night Mayhem</u>[32], Marc Gunther and Bill Carter address ABC-TV's approach to televising the NFL and old pro Frank Gifford's role: " . . . Gifford was not at all sure he liked ABC's new style of NFL coverage. To Gifford, a traditionalist to the core, the grand game of football was supreme; no fancy packaging was needed. 'I feel strongly about commentators becoming the show,' he said. 'The game of football is the event. We're strictly there to report.'

. . . Frank Gifford, a football hero of the old school, brought the values of the gilded age of the 1950's to the most revolutionary sports program ever hatched." And as I watched the first several Monday night telecasts, it was obvious that ABC Sports President Roone Arledge was bringing "show biz" to the pro football world in the "colorful" personas of Howard Cosell and "Dandy" Don Meredith—and despite what Gifford as an announcer and I as a fan may have preferred, the game was no longer the main thing. Paralleling this, musical talent was no longer the main thing to the recording industry or its partner in crime, the radio industry—glitz and glamour was.

During my "backburner" period, there were many occasions when friends would visit and I had the opportunity to shed a little sunshine with my music, which couldn't be heard anywhere else, especially on the radio—and combat this wholesale move toward hype over substance!

I remember how our friends Art and Val Shirey would come over for dinner and, with a sparkle in his eyes, Art would ask me to "put on a little Chuck Berry." "You Can't Catch Me" and "Nadine" were his favorites, and we listened for every word of Chuck's songs, nodded our heads in unison and laughed with delight at Chuck's clever writing and delivery. I've lost count of the number of hours Art and Val spent listening to Chuck and his friends.

It doesn't seem that long ago that my neighbor Don McCurry would drop by and ask me to play some of his favorites. "What Does It Take (To Win Your Love For Me)" by Junior Walker and the All Stars was his special song. After a few drinks, some shared memories, loads of music trivia, many records later Don would reluctantly leave. His standard parting words were, "They just don't make them like that anymore."

Then there was the time Don Dagenhart was in town on business and joined us for dinner. He related just how much pressure he was under at work and how it was getting to him. Out came the records and I must have played Roy Hamilton's hits "Unchained Melody" and "You'll Never Walk Alone" ten times each. Another late stayer . . . The next day he made the point of calling to tell me that the music, especially Roy Hamilton's, was like a vacation, and gave him a much needed shot in the arm.

One lunch break my boss Sandy Taylor and I were talking with some other managers when the subject of music came up. Most would single out one of the day's big stars like James Taylor as their favorite singer. Sandy, when asked who his favorite was, answered, "The Platters, I don't care for what's being played today. Give me 'Only You' over 'In The Year 2525' any day." As there wasn't much of America's golden music that could be heard on local stations, for fans like Sandy and me it truly was a dark period.

Despite that, two clubs in town, Boots' Upstairs and The Sitar, were doing turnaway business by bringing in such acts as the Drifters, the Platters, Archie Bell and the Drells, Percy Sledge, Chuck Jackson, Junior Walker and the All Stars and others. Clubs in Greenville, Charlotte, Columbia and other nearby cities were doing the same thing.

Yet throughout this time, there were almost no new recordings of

America's golden music. Stations played mainly "safe" oldies, meaning national Top 10 hits on the popular music charts—primarily those by rock artists. Radio consultants have helped keep it that way ever since. Columnist Dave Barry, in his August 23, 1992 column in the Atlanta Journal- Constitution[33] mirrored my feelings in commenting about a Shirelles' hit, " . . . I'll say 'Do vou remember a song called 'Boys?'' And Beth, instantly, will respond, 'Bop shoo-bop, boppa boppa SHOO-bop.' Then both of us, with a depth of emotion that we rarely exhibit when discussing world events, will say, 'They NEVER play that!'"

During the summer of 1972 a short news item came across my car radio that Clyde McPhatter had died. That's all there was. I never saw it in the newspaper or on television. Not one radio station carried a feature on his life or career. Wistfully I realized that never again would I hear favorites of mine like "Treasure Of Love," "Without Love," "A Lover's Question," or "Lover Please" be performed in person by Clyde.

Increasingly, 70's radio stations, both AM and FM, were ignoring America's golden music. Finally, driving my car one scorching summer day in 1976, I heard a DJ make a statement that nearly forced me off the road. It followed the rare playing of "Jim Dandy," by Lavern Baker. My pleasure was erased at record's end when the youthful, high-pitched DJ announced "There's Lavern Baker doing a song originally recorded by Black Oak Arkansas." "Jim Dandy" was a hit for Black Oak Arkansas in 1974, seventeen years after Lavern's 1957 hit.

This was typical of the gaffes about America's golden music by DJ's on the few occasions when it was played at all. The misinformation wasn't as unforgivable as the attitude with which it was usually given. It was obvious that they were bored with it, and viewed it as an intrusion. I can hear a young DJ's plea to his program director, "Man, let me play today's happening stuff. If I gotta play past hits, let me dig some Beatles or Dylan, not that stone age crap. You know?."

It seemed that even Dick Clark once felt that America's golden music was running on faded glory. When promoter Richard Nader told Clark that he wanted to hold a rock and roll revival show in 1969, Dick told Richard, as expressed in his book, Rock, Roll and Remember[34], that he "thought it was a dreadful idea." Nader then quit working for Clark and, as Clark continues to explain, "returned to New York, where he organized the first rock and roll revival shows. They did very well . . .

He'd booked a giant Fifties show in Madison Square Garden and one of the main acts had cancelled on him. He offered me a considerable amount of money to fly in to introduce the acts. I told him I didn't want to do that; if I wanted to be in that business I'd do it myself. He cajoled me a bit more and I told him I'd do it for old times' sake.

"When I walked out onstage that night at Madison Square Garden the crowd went wild. I was overwhelmed by the reaction. There was love in the air. Back in Los Angeles I couldn't get what had happened out of my head. Eventually I decided to put together my own revival show in Las Vegas."

If Dick Clark, who was a center point of this good-time music's heyday, didn't think that Richard Nader had a chance of resurrecting it in 1969, why would young DJ's have any positive feelings about this type of music? It was obvious that it would take someone who was knowledgeable about the music, but who also had a great love for it, to act as an instrument of its resurgence. I knew at that moment that I was that instrument.

A couple of months after the "Jim Dandy" incident I approached WSPA-AM radio in Spartanburg. My original idea was to provide correct information about R&B and original rock and roll, and to make my record collection available, if the station would add more of those songs to its playlist.

John Hicks, a visionary program director, finally agreed to give my concept a try. However, he suggested that I go on the air in a daily feature with one of the station's newer air personalities, Bill Curry. John's idea was to pair a local businessman who had a record collection with Curry and stage a little give-and-take about one song per day. And even though I had always gone by my middle name of Allen, or Al, I was advised not to use it on the radio, as it might hurt my insurance business. Spartanburg was an ultra conservative town and it was questioned if people would accept a radio show featuring many black R&B songs on previously almost all-white WSPA-AM. Hard to believe, but true. I used my first name, Harry, and I have been known as Harry Turner ever since. We called the show "Memory Minutes," and it ran at 5:30 p.m. Monday through Friday. The first show was broadcast in October 1976, and my "backburner" period was officially over.

It gained immediate popularity, and Bill Curry and I had a ball doing it. During one taping session in which I was featuring Clarence "Frogman" Henry singing "Ain't Got No Home," Bill totally lost it. He had never heard the record and when Clarence started singing like a frog, Bill couldn't go on, he was laughing so hard. Several takes later we "toughed" our way through it. The banter added to the appeal of the show, but despite our easy rapport, it was obvious that the music was the star. And it was readily apparent from the calls and letters that there were many people who had missed hearing the music, and were grateful to hear it again.

It didn't take long for the station to realize that their fears about using my name were unfounded. If anything, the show's popularity helped my business and, much to the station's surprise and delight, many of its biggest fans were professional people and community leaders. It pleased me as well, even though I had known all along that many listeners would "come out of the closet" and confess their enjoyment of America's golden music. When Bill Curry took another radio job early the next year, I became a solo host.

Once a week I taped an entire set of shows. On a couple of occasions, John Hicks' fiancee´, a reporter with WSPA-TV, would come in and watch me tape while waiting for John. She really seemed to love the music. I lost track of them after they got married and moved to Dallas, Texas. Then one evening I spotted her on TV and there she was—Leeza Gibbons, of "Entertainment Tonight."

The radio show had been on the air only a short time then, and I had no idea just how popular and intertwined with my life it would become. In many ways it was the beginning of the real Harry Turner.

27 Gaines, pp. 203-204.

28 Ibid., p. 214.

29 Connie Francis, *Who's Sorry Now* (New York, 1984). p. 112.

30 Ibid., p. 114.

31 Jim Ladd, *Radio Waves* (New York, 1991). pp. 236-237.

32 Marc Gunther and Bill Carter, *Monday Night Mayhem* (New York, 1988). p. 30.

33 Dave Barry, "Play some oldies, but don't turn my stomach," Atlanta *Constitution*, August 23, 1992. p. B1.

34 Clark and Robinson, p. 264.

CHAPTER 14

ON THE RADIO

My radio show had become a one-hour format that aired twice weekly. It was hard to believe the large following it had garnered. WSPA-AM was a local station, but there were phone calls and mail from all over upstate South Carolina and from neighboring areas of North Carolina and Georgia. I had always known that there was an untapped market in America's golden music, but station personnel were genuinely surprised, impressed, and pleased. The show was called "Harry Turner Presents: The Originals." It featured a combination of American music: R&B, good-time rock and roll, Carolina beach music, rockabilly, Motown, doo-wop, New Orleans music, the sounds of Philadelphia and Chicago, the blues, and surf music. I slanted the playlist toward the original artists and kept the flavor as fun-filled and down-home as possible.

What I did not play were teen idols, folk music, modern jazz or country and western. Nor was drug-related music, be it British, hard rock, Woodstock, folk rock, heavy metal or flower power music on the list. The exception to this rule would occur only if one of the songs by an artist fit one of the above categories. An example would be "Twist and Shout" by the Beatles or "Old Time Rock & Roll" by Bob Seger. Those particular recordings do justice to the R&B and good-time rock and roll sound. My concept was to give listeners an opportunity to hear music that they wouldn't normally hear on other radio stations, even with an oldies format. And I limited the play of music by superstars like Elvis because his music got so much airplay on so many other radio stations. The show was alternative radio before "alternative" was cool.

Even though normally I didn't play that much music by Elvis, there was a circumstance that overrode that fact. Late one scorching

August weekday afternoon in 1977, I stopped at a local tavern on my way home from work for a cold beer. While talking with the owner, I heard someone say that he had just heard on the radio that Elvis had been hospitalized in Memphis, and that it sounded serious. Immediately, I downed my beer and went to my car to listen to the news reports. They were sketchy at the time, but at about 5:45 P.M. I heard it announced for the first time that Elvis had been pronounced dead.

I'm sure my mouth hung agape as I just sat in my car and listened. That evening, I turned on the local TV news, and sure enough his death was confirmed. When the network news came on at 6:30, much to my surprise and consternation, it was not even the lead story. It seemed to be the ultimate evidence of the bias of American broadcast news agencies in regards to the stature of American rock and roll—America's golden music.

The next day news of Elvis Presley's death was all over radio and television, and made for banner headlines in newspapers nationwide. It was as if there were a pause by the news media hierarchy awaiting the tenor of the reaction reflected by the population in general. When the response was an overwhelming outcry by the legions of fans who idolized Elvis, the media was quick to wrap itself in the cloak of caring and concern. Ironically, it was not the "King of Rock and Roll's" unprecedented ascension to the throne, nor his tumultuous reign that made waves in the media; they didn't fully acknowledge his significance until his untimely demise.

Even though I was never a huge Elvis fan, his music was surely superior to most of what was popular in 1977, and I must admit that his death did trouble me. Elvis Presley was a part of the lives of our generation, and it was somewhat of a personal loss to many of us. As I had been on the radio for about a year when he died, I devoted my next few radio shows to his memory and received many thank yous from his fans. Theirs were some of the most heartfelt expressions of thanks that I have ever received.

Greil Marcus in his book, <u>Dead Elvis</u>[35] summed it up very well— "An exile from the real world, Elvis Presley built his own world . . . where the promise was that every fear, pain, doubt, and wish could be washed away with money, sex, drugs, and the bought approval of yesmen—Elvis Presley rotted . . . 'The moment you can do just what you like, there is nothing you care about doing.'"

I began to interview recording artists when they would be in the area, and many friendships developed. My first interview was with Archie Bell and the Drells. Their hits, "Tighten Up," "There's Gonna Be A Showdown," and "I Can't Stop Dancing" were real favorites in the Carolinas. Since I had heard Archie's jive introduction to "Tighten Up" on many occasions, I didn't know what to expect. What I found was a total surprise. I learned that in addition to singing, he was an author, a bass master fisherman, an actor, a quarter horse breeder, a gun collector, a songwriter, a dancer, a comedian, a black belt in karate, and a philosopher.

Archie's brother was University of Southern California All-American tailback, the late Ricky Bell, who had just been made the number one selection in the entire National Football League draft by the Tampa Bay Buccaneers. It is amazing that one family could produce two such diverse superstars.

Archie Bell and the Drells were mainstays in the Carolinas during the 70's, until their breakup. Their show was polished, well-choreographed, and highly entertaining. Archie had such a winning personality and a great rapport with an audience—the fans always got their money's worth and then some. Though they performed worldwide during the 60's and 70's, Archie confessed to me that the South was their "bread and butter," particularly North and South Carolina.

It was in 1977 that I first met one of my favorite R&B groups, the Clovers, with original member baritone Harold Lucas and long-time bass singer John Bowie, who joined the group in the 60's. The other two members were Johnny Mason and Roosevelt "Tippy" Hubbard. They sounded very much like the original recordings, with Tippy on lead.

The Clovers were real gentlemen and showed a genuine compassion for others. They were financially strapped, driving a dented and rusted station wagon, and had to use jumper cables to start the car. With a lump in my throat I watched them jump start the car and go out of their way to visit a young white boy named Jimmy Sharpe in the hospital in Winston-Salem, N.C. where he was slowly dying of cancer. Jimmy's mother, Betty, glows to this day as she relates how that visit was probably the highlight of Jimmy's last year of life.

When Tippy was forced to leave the group for health reasons, he was replaced by Steve Charles. Up until that time, they had been performing for the pure love of the music and the eternal belief that things would shortly get better. Steve Charles immediately improved the group, not only because of his stage presence, but because he took over as their road manager. Songs like "Devil Or Angel," "Love Potion Number 9," "Blue Velvet," and "One Mint Julep" took on a new energy and began to reach a whole new generation of fans. Then a caring manager, Mike Evans, began booking them exclusively. Rather than settling for one night stands, they found themselves performing at weekly engagements at hotels around the country, and became fixtures in Atlantic City. I watched with happiness and satisfaction, as we had become close friends.

I have particularly fond memories of the Clovers. One afternoon I was standing in my driveway talking to a neighbor, Ray Casalis, when, all of a sudden, we heard a backfiring engine and barking dogs and we spotted an old white truck that was being pursued by two large, yapping dogs. It was none other than Steve Charles, driving the Clovers' used equipment truck. He was enroute to an engagement and stopped by to say hello. Pulling into the driveway, he leaned out the window, and with a grin on his face exclaimed, "Just thought we'd stop by and ruin the neighborhood."

And I'll never forget the evening that Johnny Mason came over. He brought a bottle of Rebel Yell bourbon with him, and we pulled out a stack of records. After a few songs, Mary Ann pulled me aside to let me know that she was not at all happy, because the music was too loud. She stormed out of the room, indicating her displeasure with a reverberating door slam. As the evening wore on, the music got louder, and as we started singing along in harmony, we also got louder. At about two the next morning, and several door slams later, Johnny finally went home. The doghouse was well worth it. And to think, "One (Rebel Yell) Mint Julep" was the cause of it all!

Another group I got to know quite well was the Diamonds. Glenn Stetson's group was not an original group, but they did a good job on the Diamonds' songs like "Little Darlin'" and "The Stroll." They played occasionally at Vince Perone's Forum in Greenville, and I caught their show whenever they were in the area.

Glenn related to me a story about a performance at Vince's, when he made an innocent, lighthearted comment about Bob Jones University, a strict, fundamentalist Christian university located nearby. A man from the audience, who was obviously intoxicated, stumbled up to the front of the stage. Glenn leaned over and the man grabbed him roughly by the shirt collar, jerked him off the stage, and both tumbled to the floor. The two scuffled for a few minutes before someone finally realized it wasn't part of the act and pulled the man away from Glenn. Nobody was hurt, but Glenn remarked with a grin "I learned real fast what fundamentalist Christianity was all about."

Glenn then related what happened backstage in the dressing room after a show when a "fan" rushed up to him and exclaimed in a totally honest and innocent manner, "Gosh, I loved your show. In fact, you guys do the best job I've ever heard of singing Sha Na Na's greatest hits." Glenn remarked "I couldn't decide whether to thank him, or punch his lights out!"

The friendships and stories were just beginning . . .

A lingering dream of mine had been to bring a concert to upstate South Carolina. When promoter Rick Harp in February, 1978 asked me to be his co-promoter and to emcee a show of this type which he was planning, I jumped at the opportunity. Rick loved the music but admittedly didn't know much about it, so he needed the involvement of someone who did—and it consumed my time for the next ten weeks. The concert was to benefit the American Cancer Society and it became a real community event in April of '78. But much like Richard Nader, I was admonished by the wagging tongues and naysayers that nobody cared about America's golden music any more. These doom-and-gloomers also cautioned that the local auditorium was a risky venue for such a program, because it was old and badly in need of repair, and many out-of-towners were reluctant to attend performances there. Welcoming the challenge, I vowed to make it happen.

What a line-up we featured. The Coasters, the Diamonds, Bill Pinkney and the Original Drifters, the Clovers, and Little Anthony. When the posters were printed, I personally lugged them around town and plastered them everywhere possible—in restaurants, stores, churches, on telephone poles, trees and bus benches. Anyone was fair game for my hawking a pair of tickets. But no one, including the auditorium manager, Mike Abingdon, gave us a snowball's chance in July of meeting with success.

A month before our concert date, I had a freak accident which popped my knee out of joint. Seeking medical attention, the orthopedic surgeon told me that it was a torn cartilage, and would require surgery. I pleaded my case, telling him about the concert, how much had to be done, and how indispensable I was to the cause. It was all to no avail, so facing the inevitable, after being wheeled into surgery I peddled tickets to the anesthesiologist and his assistants before being sent into temporary oblivion.

Lying in bed with my bandaged leg, I began calling anyone and everyone connected with the concert, undeterred by surgery. The doctor had told me that I would be on crutches for six full weeks, but the concert was now less than four weeks away. Little did he know how perfectly he was feeding into my love of a challenge. After being discharged from the hospital, I planned to pick up with the details of making the concert happen, but I'd forgotten to calculate how general anesthesia would slow me down. But I vowed two things: that the concert was going to come off without a hitch and be wildly successful, and that I was going to emcee the show minus crutches. Each day I pushed myself to the point that I would pass out from fatigue by the end of the day.

Several artists were added to our original line-up of performers. Nappy Brown, singer of a 50's R&B hit, "Don't Be Angry," joined the roster. Then Joe Bennett offered to reunite his old nationally-known group the Sparkletones for an appearance. The group had a national hit, "Black Slacks," in the 50's and had appeared on both The Ed Sullivan Show and American Bandstand. I eagerly agreed, and we were set with one dynamite line-up. Area newspapers printed articles about the event, but the topper was a huge front-page article in the entertainment section of the Charlotte **Observer**. Despite the naysayers, I knew we were well on our way.

As concert time approached, I was hopping around with the aid of only one crutch. And the community was buzzing excitedly about the event. Both of Spartanburg's two top morning personalities, Bill Drake and Steve McCoy, had agreed to share emceeing chores with me, and were busily talking up the concert on the radio. Mayor Frank Allen had proclaimed the concert day as "American Cancer Society Oldies Concert Day," a fitting and appreciated gesture. The telephone was ringing off the hook with calls from people wanting tickets. Friends from all over were coming in for the concert, which added to my excitement, as I anticipated a reunion on top of the concert itself.

The hours ticked down and concert day dawned. So did a discovery which almost ruined everything. The auditorium had two separate event areas. Our concert was booked in the main auditorium, but a social club had also been booked for the downstairs area on the that same night. A group called the Original Drifters was playing for their dance. What? How could that be? We had Bill Pinkney and the Original Drifters on our show. Could they have possibly double-booked? It turned out to be a bogus group with extremely bad timing, and we quickly diffused any problems of credibility when Bill and his group arrived on the scene. Whewwww!

It was like being at a long overdue homecoming as the Drifters saw the Diamonds, who greeted the Coasters, who welcomed the Clovers, who hugged Joe Bennett and the Sparkletones and on and on. Some of the acts had not seen each other for fifteen or twenty years, and their reunion brought about an emotional high that bubbled over into the show itself. As I listened to the swapping of stories, the love and respect for one another was obvious; it was equally apparent that old professional rivalries were being awakened, and each group was eager to outdo the other. I could scarcely wait to draw the curtain on this rare occasion.

The artists had all arrived early, with the exception of Nappy Brown. The crowd also began arriving early, and it seemed each ticketholder was highly charged and brimming with anticipation. There was a special feeling, even an electricity in the air. Numerous friends came to the stage door to say "Hi." The Suggs came from Kingsport, Tennessee, the Straits from Columbia, South Carolina, the Brassells from Pickens, South Carolina. Chris Beachley brought in a group from Charlotte, North Carolina . . . it was becoming a major happening.

Shortly before the curtain rose, I received a bouquet of flowers from my father and Betty. My mother also phoned backstage to wish me well. Even though this was neither their favorite music nor was it an era they identified with, they knew how important it was to me. We were never a very demonstrative family, but the loving gestures and overt indications that evening spoke volumes.

It was time for the show to begin. I kept my promise to myself by opening the program without crutches. Few in the audience had a clue that I relied on one crutch backstage, because I never walked onstage with it. With great gusto and building excitement I brought on the first act, Joe Bennett and the Sparkletones. This hometown group sounded much as they did in the 50's, and the nostalgic crowd received them enthusiastically and gratefully. I was so happy for Joe, Howard "Sparky" Childress, Wayne Arthur and Jimmy Denton. It had always been my opinion that they were one of the best, most underappreciated rockabilly groups in history. They were extra nice guys as well. But, wait a minute . . . had anyone seen Nappy Brown?

Next on the bill were the Clovers. They were really struggling financially at the time, so it gave me goosebumps to see them put everything into their performance. The crowd was dancing in the aisles as they performed their hits. Things truly were building to a crescendo as the Clovers exited to a standing ovation. Oh boy, was it on! But no Nappy.

Little Anthony had been forced to cancel because of complications with his wife's pregnancy. No doubt one of an emcee's most dreaded duties is the announcement of a last-minute cancellation. But, as I related the facts to the audience and offered ticket refunds, they were understanding and their enthusiasm for the evening was barely dented. Not the first refund was required.

Then came the Diamonds, with Glenn Stetson singing lead. Their performance epitomized professionalism and perfect pace. Their harmony was flawless, and the crowd was out of their seats and applauding in response to each song. The Diamonds also left the stage to a standing ovation, and the excitement of the evening continued to build. But . . . not a trace of Nappy Brown.

Carl Gardner was the founder of the Coasters, and could barely contain his delight as his group did their thing. Carl was the only original member in the group, but they sounded fantastic. One of his group was none other than Earl Carroll. Earl had been the lead singer with the Cadillacs during the 50's. Today their hit "Speedoo" (singing about "Mr. Earl") is considered an uptempo doo-wop standard. Also with Carl's Coasters was Ronnie Bright, who sang bass. His claim to fame was that he was the bass voice in the background on Johnny Cymbal's 1963 hit "Mr. Bass Man." It was to an exuberant standing ovation that the Coasters exited, and their smiles radiated gratitude and a kind of awe as each member shook my hand upon passing by. But where was Nappy

Brown?

Bill Pinkney and the Original Drifters were the final act of the evening. Having both emceed and viewed Bill's and the Drifters' act on numerous occasions, I can unequivocally state that I have never seen them perform better than on that night. It was magical. Bill's salute to Drifters co-founder Clyde McPhatter charged the crowd with emotion as he offered, in his unique bass-baritone voice, Clyde's hit "Without Love." Russell Henry stilled the audience into silence as his beautiful tenor voice saluted the Platters with a breathtaking rendition of "Only You." The group was so on-the-mark that even the other entertainers gathered around just off-stage in the wings to watch their performance. From halfway through the Drifters' set until they left the stage, the entire house was standing. Remaining on their feet, the whole crowd roared their fervent approval as the Drifters closed their set. "MORE!" " MORE!" " MORE!" "MORE!" "MORE!" they chanted as they refused to let the Drifters leave the stage. I was right there, chanting "MORE" along with them, all the while wondering what could have happened to Nappy Brown.

As I walked off-stage after bringing the Drifters back for an encore, I noticed a dignified Isaac Hayes lookalike standing in the wings. He introduced himself, and said he was set to perform. Indeed it was Nappy Brown. He had gotten lost, thus his late arrival. The only problem was that he had not been able to rehearse; therefore, it was next to impossible for him to have gone out at the end and performed his set. He expressed genuine disappointment. An idea came to me. I had announced to the audience that all the performers would return at the end of the concert en masse to sing the Isley Brothers' party standard "Shout." Why not bring Nappy out, introduce him and let him lead off this grand finale? He readily agreed, and the stage was now set for a rousingly dramatic climax.

Nappy was introduced to yet another standing ovation, and the man tore into the gospel-flavored song with all his soulful might. While he was singing, Joe Bennett and the Sparkletones, the Clovers, the Diamonds, the Coasters, and Bill Pinkney and the Original Drifters were re-introduced. Concertgoers were actually hysterical, some standing in their seats. Many others were dancing in the aisles, jumping up and down, and yelling and singing along, while the various entertainers took turns singing lead and answering each other in the best gospel call-and-shout tradition. There was more love in the air than at a gospel revival. It was the same for me as it had been for Richard Nader and Dick Clark in Madison Square Garden a few years earlier. Amid the joyful finale, the curtain came down.

The once dubious auditorium manager rushed over, embraced me and gushed that the show was the greatest program he had ever been associated with, and that the talent we had all witnessed was beyond anything imaginable. Having accomplished the "impossible," I truly did savor the moment, as did the entertainers, co-promoter Rick Harp and everyone else involved. Any doubters were shown irrefutably that this beloved music was held dear and enthusiastically embraced by many people.

That evening I resolved to demonstrate this truth for all the world to witness . . .

35 Greil Marcus, *Dead Elvis* (New York, 1991). p. 48.

PART II

Artists, Friends and Remembrances

CHAPTER 15

THE CAROLINA INFLUENCE

Many areas of the country had all but abandoned their original American rock and roll and R&B roots in the wake of the British invasion. But one area of the country never forgot those roots, North and South Carolina. Carolinians have simply had a love affair with the music. With the Myrtle Beach shagging experience added to the mix, it has become a part of the Carolina lifestyle.

During the 60's, there was a club north of Myrtle Beach on Highway 17 called The Beach Club, which featured a steady stream of R&B acts. I had bought a Bo Diddley album recorded at the club in July 1963, while I was stationed at Kelly Air Force Base. Though it was a somewhat rudimentary recording, the enthusiasm for the music by the exuberant young audience was evident. The real highlight of the album for me was "On Top Of Old Smokey" done in Bo Diddley's inimitable style.

Pavilions and hang-outs along the beaches at the time still featured juke boxes full of records that kids could shag and slow dance to. The Pad at Ocean Drive, like a crusty, old sailor, smelled of stale beer, but it drew thousands of young people old enough to drink and, of course, shag on its well-worn dance floor to the pulsating rhythms of R&B music.

The shag, a simple 1-2-3, 1-2-3, 1-2 dance step, was similar to the swing or jitterbug, which derived from a dance called "the big apple", which originated in 1936 at a black nightclub called The Big Apple in Columbia, S.C. The big apple became so popular in New York City that it became the city's nickname.

But the shag was a smoother and sexier dance than either the jitterbug or the swing. Holding their partner's hand, each dancer positioned the other hand as though holding a can of beer, as was often the

112

case! The male dancer performed turns and steps in time to the music. The female partner followed, allowing the male to show-off. Summer holidays found many Carolinians joining the crowds at pavilions for some good R&B music and dancing into the wee hours of the morning. Those were the best of times!

The shag that I learned as a teenager was very different than it is now. In the shagging days of the late 40's through the 60's, having fun and dancing to favorite R&B tunes such as "Sixty Minute Man" was foremost in our minds. I think of old-time shaggers Harry Driver, Jo Jo Putnam, Betty Kennedy Cain, Billy and Wanda Jeffers, Chick Hedrick, and Jo McCaffrey who wore the floor-boards down. As the dance has evolved, new, complicated "mirror" steps have created a new breed of dancers—to the point that striving for perfection has displaced having fun. In fact, some of the old shagging "Hall of Famers" have told me that they have regretted the dance's changes from free form to "mirror step dancing" much like I have the music's changes. But it's still fun to watch shag champions Charlie Womble and Jackie McGee and free spirit dancers like Pete Gilyard, Ron Harris, Floyd and Janis Ross and Moe and Faye Patterson having a ball dancing to the music.

In the Carolinas when R&B began to be referred to as beach music in the early 70's, it cemented the connection between the music and the South Carolina coast. At that time beach music signified only R&B, most of which one could shag to. But the rush was on by competing shag DJ's to find new or obscure material to play. Enterprising individuals began to re-press records. Sometimes it was done legally from the original master, other times it would be bootlegged from a clean 45. Many of the artists never got a penny from these new pressings. It's hard to break the endless circle when money is involved.

As beach music grew in popularity during the 80's, there were a couple of disturbing developments. Dancers began shagging to country and western, disco, and pop music records, in addition to R&B as long as they contained the mandatory 120 beats per minute. The dance began to dictate the music rather than the other way around. The shag is one of the only dances to have drifted away from the music from which it was spawned. What had made the dance so irresistible was its musical R&B roots and the fun times the music afforded.

About the same time, regional horn bands began to supplant the original artists. It disturbed me to see groups who had never had anything other than regional hits, get concert billing over artists with national hits, like the Tams—simply because they were the right color, good looking, and had the right connections. Just as Elvis and the Beatles took the play away from black R&B singers in the 50's and 60's, so too have imitators in the Carolinas since the 70's.

Still beach music reigns supreme in the Carolinas. There have been bi-annual S.O.S. shagging events since the early 80's that draw thousands of shaggers from all over the country to North Myrtle Beach. Shaggers become teenagers all over again, reliving the glory of the early days. Shag clubs literally dot the landscape in the Carolinas and have been spreading to other neighboring states. In North and South Carolina some radio stations have dedicated their entire formats to Carolina beach music, several syndicated beach music radio shows have sprung up, and there are numerous locally produced ones. Beach music popularity charts have sprung up and are updated periodically.

The shag was declared the official state dance of South Carolina by the state legislature, thanks to super music and shagging fan, Legislator Bubber Snow. There have been four Carolina beach music awards shows, three of which were televised nationally. Of course, my old favorites have continued to perform in the Carolinas—and many a time, I have seen a sign advertising Bill Pinkney and the Original Drifters, the Clovers, Maurice Williams and the Zodiacs, the Swinging Medallions, Billy Scott, Clifford Curry, Archie Bell, or the Tams, and my car has come to a screeching halt.

Hosting a radio show and promoting live concerts led me into the "Dirty Dancing" phenomenon when I received an intriguing call from the mountain resort town of Lake Lure, N.C. in 1986. The call was from John Mojjis, the new owner of the fabled Lake Lure Inn. John and Betty Mojjis had recently purchased the inn, which was located within sight of Lake Lure. The old inn, with its wide porticoes and welcoming rocking chairs, had a certain charm and character. A movie production company had contacted John and his wife Betty about using the inn as a cast and crew headquarters for a location shoot at Lake Lure. John not only worked out terms for the film crew's stay, but convinced them to shoot many of the movie's scenes on picturesque property in close proximity to the inn.

The excitement and publicity the movie was generating led John to some unique entertainment ideas to draw more people to Lake Lure. The result was "Swingfest," a combination of big band and America's golden music, and it became an annual summer event. It was my pleasure to emcee the artists, as they were some of my favorites.

The line-up for the first concert in 1987 consisted of Archie Bell, Maurice Williams and the Zodiacs, Carla Thomas, the Dell Vikings, the Clovers and Shag Time (a local beach music group). Good-time DJ Tony Union played in between sets, so that the music was non-stop. The highlight of the evening came when the Clovers, Dell Vikings, and Carla got on stage together for a jam session. I still remember the words of the late Kripp Johnson of the Dell Vikings who exclaimed, "Harry, the atmosphere here is the closest thing I remember to the old Alan Freed concerts in the 50's. This 'Swingfest' thing is awesome!"

R&B legends were featured at the inn on weekends including Bill Pinkney and the Original Drifters, Hank Ballard and the Midnighters, the Moonglows, Marv Johnson, the Flamingos, the Platters, Frankie Ford, the Orioles, Billy Scott, the Showmen, the Orlons, and the Shirelles among others.

Just after the film's shooting was completed, John asked me to DJ and MC at the cast extras' party after the film's premiere in Hendersonville, N.C. The film was about dancing in the early 60's, but few even knew it's title at the time. And until the premiere showing of "Dirty Dancing," I had no idea that most of the music in the movie was America's golden music.

At the party, everyone was jubilant, as the movie looked like it was going to be a smash. John gave me a copy of the soundtrack album which contained only a portion of the songs in the movie. Although the obvious highlight of the movie was it's theme song, "I've Had The Time Of My Life," by Bill Medley and Jennifer Warnes, I received the most requests that evening for "Cry To Me," by Solomon Burke which played when actors Patrick Swayze and Jennifer Grey were making love for the first time. Luckily I had a copy of the song with me as it was not on the album.

No one that evening had any idea just how successful the enjoyable, but little publicized movie was to become. "Dirty Dancing" soon became a cult classic, with some fans viewing the movie over 100 times.

Thousands came to Lake Lure to visit the site where it had been filmed.

The soundtrack album quickly became a smash and sold well in excess of 10,000,000 copies. I was emceeing Maurice Williams and the Zodiacs when the film's writer presented Maurice with a platinum album for his hit "Stay" on the soundtrack album. Maurice told me that he made more money from "Stay" on the soundtrack than when it was a number one hit in 1960! RCA released a "More Dirty Dancing" album, containing the remaining soundtrack songs, including "Cry To Me." It also sold several million copies. Songs from the film, both original and new, became hits. "Do You Love Me," by the Contours, a top ten hit in 1962, became a top ten hit all over again.

When the movie was released on videotape, it immediately became a best seller and number one rental. "Dirty Dancing" contests became the rage. All of this was done with little promotion—the nostalgic feel of the story, Patrick and Jennifer's charisma, the music and the dancing all combined to give "Dirty Dancing" all the promo it needed. The movie showed kids how much fun the music and dancing could be. For a brief time the generation gap narrowed.

About the same time an idea took root that turned Lake Lure Inn into a real showplace. I had heard about a local North Carolina group called the "Golden Sounds Of Motortown," which performed the type of music featured on my radio show. Merwin Gross, the group's producer, invited me to attend a performance. The show's professionalism surprised me. The singers and musicians were first-rate. I suggested to John that he bring them to Lake Lure. The crowd's response to "Motortown's" first show at Lake Lure Inn was overwhelming, and it was a marriage made in heaven.

For weeks, John's property had been besieged by fans wanting to see "Baby's bridge," "the cabin" and other film sites—there was even a waiting list of people wanting to sleep overnight in the room where Patrick Swayze stayed during filming. That's when John and Merwin then came up with the idea of a "Dirty Dancing Revue." It combined "The Golden Sounds Of Motortown" with a choreographed show featuring some of the original dancers from the movie and music from the soundtrack. Each week-end the rustic pavilion where the movie's dance scenes had been filmed was packed to capacity with enthusiastic fans. The show captured the very essence of the movie and it clicked right from the start. It was like we all had been transported to a magical moment in time. Merwin and his show became mainstays in the area for several years, performing for visitors from all over the country.

The show was eventually taken on the road, and John asked me to emcee it on its upstate stop. Maurice Williams and the Zodiacs were added to the line-up to strengthen its appeal. There were about a thousand people in the audience, the majority of whom were young girls between the ages of 5 and 20. They all sat in bleachers around the arena's edge, with a big dancing area between the bleachers and the stage.

Maurice and the Zodiacs led off the show. The third song in their set was the Little Richard classic, "Tutti Frutti." When Maurice began singing, the girls in the audience rushed to the front of the stage, screaming and singing along with every word! He broke into the Coasters' hit "Yakety Yak", and the girls screamed in unison, "Don't talk back!" Maurice came back for three or four encores before the crowd let him off the stage. Maurice told me later, "Harry, I felt like a teenage singer all over again!" The generation gap closed that night.

The actual "Dirty Dancing Review" was well received that evening, but Maurice and his group had already wrung the crowd dry. Again and again I've found that when young people attend an America's golden music concert, they capture its energy, honesty, soulfulness, and fun-filled nature for themselves. Maurice Williams and the Zodiacs had proven it one more time.

The show had a successful, regional tour. But once the "Dirty Dancing" experience had faded into a pleasant memory, the Lake Lure Inn fell on hard times. The inn was sold and John and Betty moved to Florida. However, those memories can never be replaced.

John and Betty along with other Carolinians, with their love for America's golden music, and a dogged determination to do their own thing, have shown the rest of the country how to keep the substance and fun alive. There is something to be admired about people who stick to their roots. Long live the Carolinas, Carolina beach music, and the shag!

CHAPTER 16

MR. GOLDEN PIPES

Music has the power to cross all kinds of boundaries. As a young boy, it never entered my mind that I would have the opportunity to meet the artists on the shiny, new records I bought and treasured. As time would tell, some unforgettable artists and friends changed my life and added a whole new dimension. One of those special people was John R.

While spending summers and week-ends in Ware Shoals I had become acquainted with an extra special radio station. It was 50,000 watt, clear channel WLAC-AM that beamed out of Nashville, Tennessee to which my friends and I listened almost every night. This was in the time before FM radio, when the DJ's were as important as the music they played. WLAC gave us the best of both. My favorite announcer in the mid-50's was Gene Nobles. He hosted the popular "Randy's Record Shop Show," which featured music from the store's mail order specials and was a co-owner of the shop. These specials offered six hit 45's for a fraction of the local store retail price. I bought records from Randy's during the 50's and always got a real charge when they arrived in my mailbox. Since Randy's primary owner, Randy Wood, owned Dot Records, Gene always found a way to include a Dot label record or two in each special offer. In many ways it was the precursor of television and radio pitches encouraging viewers and listeners to ". . . call now 1-800-. . . use your credit card, and you too, can own . . ."

Nobles also did an hour show that followed, on which he was joined by "Cohort 6 and 7/8s" and his Tarzan yell. He was a master of double entendré. His favorite subject was how the strippers at Nashville's Rainbow Club reminded him of "Oldsmobiles with big head-lights coming straight at you." "Droopy drawers music" was his term ascribed to romantic, slow-dance ballads. The highlight of his second hour show was his nightly live delivery, always slightly risqué, of the commercial for White Rose Petroleum Jelly. We loved it! Combined with his penchant for sexual innuendo, Gene Nobles played what we felt was the best combination of music aired by any radio announcer in the U.S.A., and my friends and I were hooked! When word was spreading about the upcoming ABC-TV rock and roll TV show, American Bandstand, I just knew that its host would be Gene Nobles. It had to be— he was the best!

But Nobles, not in very good health, retired a couple of years later—much to our chagrin. He was replaced by Hugh "Baby" Jarrett, a member of Elvis' backup group, the Jordanaires. While Hugh's show was at its peak, I was in Columbia at school and couldn't pick up the station unless I was traveling so I didn't hear him that often, and was never that familiar with his shows. Hugh now lives in Atlanta and we have become friends.

There was a show which came on earlier in the evening, the blues-oriented, "Ernie's Record Shop Show," hosted by a leather-lunged DJ named John Richbourg. I didn't listen to it quite as much since I wasn't as big a fan of blues music as pure R&B. Still, I would flip my car radio to WLAC whenever possible. The one constant thread was the ever present voice of John R. More and more, I became a fan of the man as the 60's wore on. It was obvious how much he cared for R&B and blues. But even more apparent was his concern for the artists themselves. Never risqué, he was always a gentleman and his life was his music. So during the 60's John R. became my main WLAC man.

In 1982 I became involved in another concert effort. Eager to come up with something unique for the concert, I learned that John R. was still alive. "Aha! Why not invite John R. to come and help emcee the concert?" I called WLAC and was able to locate John R. through the assistance of Bill "Hoss" Allen, another of the long-time WLAC R&B and gospel DJ's. When I got John on the line and told him of my idea, he said he would be delighted to do it, but indicated that he was not in good financial shape due to health problems. Since the concert was for charity, funds were limited; however, John quickly agreed to come for expenses and a little pocket money. I would finally get to meet this special man.

Word quickly spread among his fans that John R. was coming. Even artists like the Tams and the Clovers, whom he had helped over the years, were like kids about seeing the radio legend again. When I met him, I couldn't believe it was John R., as he couldn't have weighed over 100 pounds. I wondered to myself how that resonant baritone voice could have originated within that small frame. But when the man spoke, there was no doubt that it was indeed the voice so revered by multitudes of Southern rock and roll, blues, and R&B fans.

That evening John taped a radio show with me for broadcast the following Sunday afternoon. Awed station personnel were respectful of his presence, and several, including Tony Brooks, the station owner, asked for his autograph. The radio show was one of the best I have ever done—John spoke candidly about his career, his love for the artists and their music, and the inequities and indignities that they faced through the years. It was clear that John had done all he could to promote them, and it was with sadness that he spoke of the fates that had befallen many of his artist friends.

In all my years on the radio, the end of the taping with John was the only time I have ever gotten emotional on the air. I knew that the cancer ravaging his body would not allow him many more years. As I thanked this warm, caring, humble and infinitely giving man, I could scarcely get the words out.

As we milled around backstage at the concert, John R. was effervescent as he saw entertainer friends for the first time in years, and was besieged by fans for autographs. I introduced John to South Carolina Comptroller General Earle Morris, who had driven up all the way from Columbia for the show and especially to meet John. Earle was an old friend and long time supporter of my efforts to promote and preserve this music.

Introducing John to the audience and bringing him onstage to a standing ovation was another moment of overwhelming emotion. It was a night of admiration and love on the part of the artists, the fans and the promoters for the man everyone simply knew as John R. He told me after the concert that it was one of the highlights of his life, and thanked me over and over again.

When I saw John R. off for his return trip to Nashville, I felt as if I were saying good-bye for the last time. But, fortunately that was not to be the case. We stayed in touch by phone for the next couple of years, knowing that his health was deteriorating progressively. He had become almost incapacitated, though he never complained. I had no idea just how bad the situation was until I received a call from a woman in Atlanta named Dell Long. She was organizing a benefit concert in Nashville to help John with his mounting medical bills. I was able to help line up some artists from the Carolinas, and she confirmed that it would take place at the Grand Ole Opry in March of 1985.

There was no way I could possibly have missed that show, as I had grown very close to the gentle man with the golden pipes. It turned out to be one of the greatest evenings of my life and the artist roster was unbelievable. Wolfman Jack emceed the show, and the legendary Jack the Rapper emceed the awards banquet. James Brown, B.B. King, the Charlie Daniels Band, the Neville Brothers, Ruth Brown, Hank Ballard, Carla Thomas, Maurice Williams and the Zodiacs, John Conlee, Billy Scott, the Coasters, the Tams, Rufus Thomas, Ella Washington, Joe Simon and others performed—and for expenses only. They were backed by an all-star band featuring the Memphis Horns.

John R. was born in Kingstree, S.C., so I was on hand to present a proclamation from the South Carolina state legislature. I was backstage throughout the program and met all of the entertainers I didn't already know. Country and Western pioneer Roy Acuff did not perform on the show, but thoroughly enjoyed milling around backstage and watching the festivities. It was truly a page of music history—with James Brown, the king of soul, B.B. King, the king of the blues, and Roy Acuff, the king of country music all backstage together. I was in Rufus Thomas' dressing room when Rufus and Roy Acuff met for the first time—it was a mutual admiration society in 3D and living color as they swapped reminiscences.

Artist after artist sang their hearts out for the man who helped launch so many careers. Dell Long had pulled off one amazing show! It was the first time R&B music was ever performed on the Grand Ole Opry stage, and it was all carried out with great aplomb, in a special, loving manner. Though all the artists were in rare form that night, I'll never forget sitting in the audience with Maurice Williams and watching the "Bear Cat," Rufus Thomas all but steal the show with his thoroughly disarming clowning and showmanship. The old man gave everybody a lesson that night. All the artists assembled on-stage for a grand finale which left everyone misty-eyed. With deeply felt emotion, I knew that that evening would be the last time I would see John R.

John and I did talk by phone several times afterward. Even though I knew that his life was slipping away, it was terribly difficult to take the news of his death when I received the call from Dell. John R. selflessly gave of himself and made a positive difference in countless lives—my own included.

CHAPTER 17

THE FAT MAN FROM NEW ORLEANS

Fats Domino got his start in his hometown of New Orleans, Louisiana—one of the world's most musical cities. His first record, "The Fat Man," was released on the Imperial label in 1949, and was an immediate hit on the race music chart. From that first success he became a consistent chart topper on the race chart, and its successor the rhythm and blues chart. Fats had been recording for about six years before I heard "Ain't It A Shame." Fats', however, was not the first version of the song that I had heard. It had been covered by Pat Boone, and played on the white stations in Greenville. Pat's version was catchy, but when I heard the original and obviously superior version by Fats Domino, I was hooked!

This was at the beginning of the cover record era. The next song by Fats was "Bo Weevil," which was covered by an old favorite of mine, Teresa Brewer, as I had loved her version of "Music, Music, Music." One sure sign that an artist was hot was when he had several records covered by other artists. Record companies wasted little time in getting their mass marketable artists into the studio to record a version of a hot artist's song. A **Time** magazine article title from the 50's on Fats said it best—"Fats on Fire," because at the time, Fats was figuratively burning up the record charts.

The years 1955 to 1962 saw an almost unbroken string of hits from Fats on the pop chart. His crossover was accomplished in short order. He was more readily acceptable to whites than many of his contemporaries because he was non-threatening—he was heavy set, cute like a teddy bear, and had a good nature about him. Fats was never an outrageous, rebellious or sexy entertainer, so he was fairly "safe". But his music was so catchy, it simply sold and sold and sold—he totally deserved his place on the charts.

His hits during his heyday read like a who's who of music:

"Blueberry Hill"
"Bo Weevil"
"I'm In Love Again"
"I'm Walkin'"
"Ain't It A Shame"
"Sick And Tired"
"My Blue Heaven"
"Blue Monday"
"When My Dreamboat Comes Home"
"Whole Lotta Lovin'"
"I Want To Walk You Home"
"I'm Gonna Be A Wheel Someday"
"Be My Guest"
"Walking To New Orleans"
"Jambalaya"
"Let The Four Winds Blow"
"Valley Of Tears"
"My Girl Josephine"
"Three Nights A Week"

Fats came to the Greenville area on several occasions and my friends and I never missed a concert. The first time we saw him was on Halloween night 1956, just after the release of "Blueberry Hill," which went on to become his biggest hit. Whites were seated in the balcony and we watched blacks dancing on the main floor—were they ever having a good time! As he broke into the refrains of some of his earlier R&B hits like "Goin' To The River," "Please Don't Leave Me," "The Fat Man," "Poor Me," "Ain't It A Shame," "I'm In Love Again," and "My Blue Heaven," there were squeals of excitement from the ladies below for their favorite songs because they were so infectious.

In 1957, while "Blue Monday" was still riding high on both the R&B and pop charts, a rumor started that Fats had throat cancer, had only a very short time to live, and that he was going to release one more record as a farewell to his fans. We fans waited and wondered until the next release actually hit the record stores. It was entitled "Valley Of Tears," and upon listening to it we just knew it had to be a farewell, sure

124

enough, and we were heartbroken. But much to our relief, we learned shortly thereafter that it was only a rumor. The Fat Man lived heartily on, his string of hits continued, and his faithful fans, like me, bought every one.

Louis Machen, a projectionist at the theater where I worked, was the operator of the lighting board at Greenville's Textile Hall when concerts came there. So whenever we attended a concert, at intermission we would go backstage to talk to Louis. On one occasion, I heard the sound of a spirited dice game with active wagering on the other side of some curtains. Out of curiosity, I stepped aside so I could take a look, and there was Fats, having quite a time shooting craps with other troupe members while waiting for his set to begin.

At my high school Fats was the favorite artist among us guys who were rock and roll and R&B fans. Girls liked Fats but were more into the cute and sexy type of singers. One particular day when some of us were watching a racial disturbance on TV, one of the guys commented, "They ought to shoot those n———." I was surprised by his racist comment, as he was a Fats Domino fan and it seemed so out of character. I wasted no time and asked, "If Fats Domino was in the front of that group, what would you do?' He paused for a second, and retorted, "They'd have to shoot me first!"

My parents' reactions to Fats' music were varied. My father liked his music somewhat. After all, Fats had a pretty good-sized orchestra featuring several horns, and his music shared a kinship with one of Dad's favorite music types, New Orleans jazz. It gave him a certain comfort level. Mother, on the other hand, didn't like his music one bit. R&B and rock and roll were both an affront to her tastes, and in her opinion, had no redeeming value. When she entered my bedroom to find pictures of Fats and other rock and roll singers tacked to my walls, she considered this downright perverse, but it mattered not at all to me. Fats and I were going to change the world!

In 1968, I met Fats for the first time while he was performing in the lounge at the Flamingo Hotel and Casino in Las Vegas. Mother's favorite female vocalist, Ella Fitzgerald, was playing in the main room of the Flamingo. Imagine my delight when Ella walked into the lounge for Fats' performance. Considering that Mother felt Ella's music was vastly superior to Fats', she never could have believed that Ella would lower herself to associate with him. At the end of his show, Ella joined Fats at his table. I went over and got Fats' and Ella's autograph on one napkin. It was with great satisfaction that I presented my mother with the napkin with Ella's autograph, then unfolded it to reveal Fats' autograph on the other side. The expression on her face was one of amused disbelief.

Today Fats plays selective engagements, often in Europe where he is revered. He still sounds just like he did during the 50's—the warm laughs, knowing smiles, eager hand-claps, standing ovations, and even wistful tears of his audiences attest to the love for this great artist. When Fats is at the grand piano and dips his shoulder, it tells everyone how into the music he is. Fats and his orchestra members still dress in sharp-looking suits and tuxedos. Synthesizers are not part of Fats' orchestra—it is the real thing, horns and all. Herbert Hardesty, sax soloist with Fats for forty years, and other band members still blow the house down. Fats simply bangs the piano and sings his numerous hits. Recently, when I interviewed this great musical legend backstage between bites of his favorite red beans and rice, unlike what I would have expected, he was a most unassuming, almost shy gentleman.

Talmadge Stuckey, the owner of the old Capricorn Studio in Macon, Georgia joined his brother Eugene, Ron Rich and me for a recent trip to Bay St. Louis, Mississippi to see Fats perform at Casino Magic's first anniversary celebration. We sat with Clarence "Frogman" Henry backstage and were transported along with about 5500 other fans straight back to the 50's. As the crowd rollicked through Fats' performance and gave him a standing ovation for the entire last portion of the show, it was obvious just how good Fats, Herbert Hardesty and the whole bunch were. It was also obvious just how well it brought people together—it was one happy crowd!

An episode of the television series, "Knots Landing" tells the real feelings of millions of fans about Fats when character Gary Ewing sang joyously along with Fats on his recording of Ain't It A Shame." "Who is that singer?" asks his son on the show. "That's Fats Domino," Gary emphatically answers. "Is Fats Domino still alive?" Gary Ewing replies, "Son, Fats Domino will never die."

CHAPTER 18

"BOOM BOOM"

During American Bandstand's early days—the late 50's and the early 60's, the mainstays of the program were the "teen idols"-Fabian, Frankie Avalon, Paul Anka, Sal Mineo, and Bobby Rydell The one female singer was Connie Francis. Fabian, Frankie, Bobby, and Connie were from the Philadelphia area where American Bandstand originated. Paul and Sal, though not from Philly, were apparently viewed as special by the show's producers and Dick Clark himself. Although they were selected mainly for their looks and sex appeal, Bobby Rydell, Paul Anka, and Connie Francis had as much talent as looks. Indeed, Anka demonstrated such singing and song writing ability, that he has endured very well—having penned the unofficial Frank Sinatra theme song, "My Way" as well as the theme song on "The Tonight Show With Johnny Carson." They were also my favorites of the teen idols featured on American Bandstand. But there was another artist who stood out most of all to me—Freddy Cannon.

With a name like Cannon, the nickname "Boom Boom" was probably to be expected, so he was usually introduced as " . . . Freddy Boom Boom' Cannon!" But "Boom Boom" would still have been appropriate for the driving beat behind most of his records. Even though Freddy was an American Bandstand regular, I never considered him to be a teen idol. He had too much talent. After all, my turn-on simply was the beat of his up tempo good-time rock and roll. "Tallahassee Lassie," "Way Down Yonder In New Orleans," "Action," "Abigail Beecher," and his biggest hit, "Palisades Park," all "boom boomed" infectiously into one's bones. When the term good-time rock and roll is mentioned, Freddy comes to my mind as the best of the "good-time rock and rollers." Freddy would be the first to tell you that he doesn't have the greatest voice, but given

127

his ability to rock and roll, it doesn't matter. Through the years I have collected most of his records, and for one reason—they were great rock and roll records.

During the 60's and 70's Freddy made an occasional appearance on television, mostly on shows produced by Dick Clark. When the television game show "The Gong Show" was in its heyday during the 70's Freddy made a few appearances as a guest panelist. Game show producer ("The Dating Game," "The Honeymoon Game," and "The Gong Show) Chuck Barris had been the songwriter of Freddy's hit "Palisades Park." Because of his contacts and friendships with Dick Clark and Chuck Barris, Freddy was more visible than many of the 50's and 60's artists over the years.

I had not seen him in person since his appearance at the Greenville Memorial Auditorium in 1959. Because of the success of my first live rock and roll show in 1978, I decided to bring another show to the upstate of South Carolina in 1979. When I began checking with booking agents about available artists for the show, I was informed about a Bo Diddley-Freddy Cannon joint booking at a special price. Almost immediately, I gave the agency the green light to book them. From the previous year's show I brought back the popular groups, Bill Pinkney and the Original Drifters and the Clovers to round out the bill.

Leading off the show, his performance rocked the house, and set the "boom boom" tempo for the rest of the performers. When the show ended, Freddy pulled me aside and asked if I could help him work a deal with a local hotel so he could stay over for a few days before the next week-end's performance in the Northeast. Talk about slick! I took Freddy to the local Sheraton where he promptly worked out a free room in exchange for doing some promotion for the hotel. Since he was in the area, we spent a good bit of time together, and he co-hosted my radio show. In my seventeen years on the air, that show stands out along with the Dee Clark, Marv Johnson, John Richbourg, and Hank Ballard shows as the best I have ever done.

Minutes into the show it was apparent how knowledgeable Freddy was about America's golden music. He sang along on the air with Chuck Berry's "Roll Over Beethoven." After I played "Ain't It A Shame," by Fats Domino, Freddy got on the air and said, "After hearing that record by Antoine Fats Domino, how can anybody go out and buy the same record by Pat Boone." When I played "Tutti Frutti," by Little Richard, he opined, "Harry, they ought to take every Pat Boone record of that song and melt them down so they can re-press them into Little Richard's version." Freddy Cannon certainly held back no opinions! When I told him that the Drifters did the original versions of both "Ruby Baby" and "Drip Drop," he was flabbergasted as he had thought that Dion (who had hits later with both songs) was the original artist and had written the songs. A clearly upset Freddy told my radio audience, "Harry, I don't want to get angry about this, but I have been on shows with Dion when he informed the audience that he did the original versions and even that he wrote them." [Both songs were penned by legendary songwriters Jerry Lieber and Mike Stoller]. He then told the radio audience, "The next time I perform with Dion and hear him make the claims that he did the original versions and wrote those two songs, I will go out on-stage and embarrass him in front of the audience by telling the truth."

Freddy's conviction that the original artists were the best of the rock and roll artists and had been blatantly stolen from, was also quite obvious. His favorite artist of all time is "Big" Joe Turner, and he reminds me of that fact even to this day. A friend of mine saw Freddy perform in Las Vegas and told me that Freddy sang "Shake, Rattle, and Roll" during his performance and told the audience, "I don't sing it like Bill Haley and the Comets (who covered the record and had a bigger hit than Joe Turner's original version), I do it like my hero, 'Big' Joe Turner." Sure enough when I saw Freddy in Atlanta a few years ago, that's exactly what he said.

During his stay in the area, he came over for dinner on several occasions, and entertained the neighborhood kids for hours with his World Champion yo yo tricks. I was sorry to see him go when I took Freddy to the airport a few days later.

In 1980 I got an excited call from Freddy telling me that he was performing at the South Carolina Peach Festival along with Bobby Rydell and Danny and the Juniors. We invited him to stay at our home, and he readily accepted. He also told me that he was about to release a new record with the Belmonts (formerly Dion's group) called, "Let's Put The Fun Back In Rock and Roll." With its release shortly thereafter, Freddy was again on the Top 100 charts and was one happy camper when we picked him up at the airport a few weeks later.

He asked if I would accompany and chauffeur him to the concert. In past years I had emceed Peach Festival concerts, but since I was not involved that year I decided to relax and enjoy the show. So what did Freddy do? He took the stage and spent—what seemed like forever—talking about his friend, Harry Turner. The concert promoter, whom I knew, came over to me and in no uncertain terms informed me that he did not appreciate Freddy promoting me more than the festival itself. However, Freddy gave his usual "boom boom" rocking performance and after the show I told him about the promoter's anger, he poo-pooed the entire scenario, and said, "Anytime I get a chance to promote one of my friends, I'm going to do just that, and if they don't like it, they can lump it."

Several years went by without seeing Freddy, then in 1986 I received a call from him telling me that he was going to be appearing at the Fox Theatre in Atlanta with Fats Domino and several other acts. I drove down with tape recorder in hand to get interviews with those on the show. I was talking with Frankie Ford and Bo Diddley's daughter backstage between interviews when I heard this commotion behind the stage curtain. Who else? It was good ole Freddy entertaining Fats Domino's band with his variety of yo yo tricks. The guys were in stitches! After the show I joined Freddy, Frankie, Lesley Gore, and Fats at the lounge at their hotel, and Freddy again kept us all entertained.

The most recent time I saw Freddy was in Kissimmee, Florida when he appeared at the opening of Little Darlin's Rock and Roll Palace along with Frankie Ford and the Diamonds. Freddy opened the show. (He may be the best opening act in rock and roll as "the man who never met a stranger" always gets things off to a rollicking good start. But he also performs well in the middle of a show, or at a show's end). He kept telling the audience how happy he was to be in Orlando again. One slightly inebriated fan was highly offended that Freddy wouldn't say that he was in Kissimmee, instead of Orlando. Unruffled, Freddy informed the audience that "I'm singing the next song, 'Palisades Park' for everyone in the audience except that guy who keeps yelling about Kissimmee." The audience cheered lustily and hard.

Freddy Cannon is one of the true free spirits in rock and roll. He will never hesitate to stand up for what he believes and speak his mind. Yet this same opinionated, principled man can "boom boom" an audience like almost no other rock and roller.

While together Freddy related a story about a concert where he was performing with Frankie Avalon, Fabian, and Bobby Rydell. All three others gave smoother and more sophisticated, yet less rocking performances than Freddy's. But Freddy stole the show and left the audience calling for more. One of the other three—Freddy didn't say which—walked up to him after his performance and told him that he was nothing but a'white n———! Freddy related further, "I looked him directly in the eye and replied, 'Thank you.'" He then told me that it had been meant as an insult, but his fellow singer had in fact just given him one hell of a compliment. That's my buddy Boom Boom!

CHAPTER 19

THE GOVERNOR

One of the best times of my life was when I worked at the Carolina and Center theaters in high school in Greenville as an usher with Larry Batson, Monty Tucker, Richard Brassell, Jim Seel, Richard Hill, Ken Bowen, George Davis, John Collins, Bill Collins, Paul Flowe, Margaret Trussell, Randy Smith, Anna Garreaux, Lewis Machen, Toy Sizemore, Billie Mitchell, Hazel Arnie, plus Mr. Guthrie, Mr. Pettit, Ms. Bull and Ted Bruce at the Fox.

The pranks we got away with were something else—like Monty sitting by himself in the front row of the theatre and talking out loud to the characters in the movie or taking a feather duster and leaning over the back row rail to dust the heads of bald-headed audience members—then hiding!

Of all the girls that worked with us ushers, none was better looking than Iris at the Center Theater. She was untouchable, as she had a steady boyfriend, a school friend of mine named Carroll Campbell, but we still thought that she was something special. Iris became my advisor to the lovelorn, explaining the necessary little nuances that were unique to each girl that I dated. She had a great sense of humor and loved to have fun.

The normal pre-movie music fare consisted of what has since become known as "elevator music." One Sunday, Chastain, the projectionist told Iris and me that he had only a couple of records to play before the movie began. But as he needed more music, even though rock and roll and R&B were taboo, I dashed out to my car and brought in some of my 45's for him to play. I handed him a stack of records which would

132

pass muster, but, in the middle of the stack, I inserted a Fats Domino record. Imagine the positive reaction Fats got from the moviegoers, as something up tempo and high-spirited played amidst the typical waltzy schmaltzy songs of the day! Iris and I were literally dancing in the lobby, if only for a few moments.

I had been out of touch with Iris, and had no idea of what had become of her. When I began hearing of a politician-on the-rise in Greenville named Carroll Campbell, and saw him interviewed on television, it turned out to be Iris' old boyfriend and my old schoolmate. He had become a statewide political force. During the late 70's, he ran for Congress, and since his district included my home county, I began actively campaigning for him in his race against the popular mayor of Greenville, Max Heller. I drove him around the upstate area to introduce him to potential backers. Carroll won the Congressional seat, and later became the Governor of South Carolina. My former lovelorn advisor Iris became the First Lady.

Carroll Campbell has always had a deep and abiding love of America's golden music. He has co-hosted some vignettes about the music which were featured on my "Memory Minutes" radio show. He has cut radio spots for concerts I have promoted, and he and Iris have attended every one they possibly can. Carroll even emceed the Clovers' performance at one show in Greenville. He walked on-stage without notes and introduced each of the Clovers by name, then reeled off about ten of their hits. Both the audience and the Clovers were amazed. Carroll and his son, Mike, spent an hour or two backstage in the dressing room talking with the Clovers about their music.

The Governor's love for this music began during the days of one of the original race music stars, Amos Milburn. During World War II, Amos had been a steward on a ship captained by Carroll Campbell's father. In fact, Captain Campbell and his mates gave Amos the first piano he ever owned. During the early 50's Amos came to Greenville with an all-black review and Carroll went with his father to see and meet Amos. The Governor related, "We were about the only two white people in the place, and it stands out as one of the highlights of my life." Whenever I play music at an event for Governor Campbell, I must be sure to have Amos Milburn's "Chicken Shack Boogie" and "One Scotch, One Bourbon, One Beer" in my record stack.

133

At a Charleston campaign rally during his gubernatorial race in 1986, I was emceeing and spinning records and my buddy Maurice Williams and the Zodiacs were performing. During their performance, Carroll came over and began talking to me. He always has been extremely neat, with every hair in place, almost a walking ad for <u>Gentleman's</u> <u>Quarterly</u> magazine. It seemed as though he were subtly guiding me toward the far end of the large room, near a set of stairs. He whispered to me that he thought he might have a hole in his pants, and asked if I minded checking. Yep, there it was, right in the seat of his trousers. Smoothly, almost imperceptibly, he backed up the stairs. A couple of minutes later, the hole repaired, he casually appeared, gave me a wink to acknowledge our little secret, and waded back into the crowd of supporters.

Throughout my life I have met and become friends with people in public office, but nothing compares with an experience during the presidential campaign of 1988. The Governor was serving as Vice President George Bush's Southern campaign chairman, and his people recruited me to emcee a rally for Bush to be held at the University of South Carolina at Spartanburg. It took place just a few days before Super Tuesday, and was well run, with two exceptions. The Vice-President was running late, and despite expectations of crowds numbering in the thousands, only a few hundred people showed up. My job became trickier, as I had to keep the restless crowd entertained while we awaited Vice-President Bush's arrival. There were bands and other entertainment on hand, and we worked them all feverishly. Still, I had lots of time to fill, and had to keep them charged up. By the time the Vice-President, Governor Campbell, and their entourage arrived, the modest-sized crowd was at a fever pitch. It was still anybody's guess as to who would win the election, so an enthusiastic crowd was vitally important.

Before I went on-stage for the actual introduction ceremonies, I met with the Vice-President backstage. We talked for a couple of minutes alone before Governor Campbell joined us. Bush was a genuinely nice person, and was truly interested in my work with the music. Governor Campbell had spoken to the Vice President about my radio show and the music I featured, but thanks to his campaign chairman, the late Lee Atwater, he had already developed an understanding and appreciation of it. (Lee had played guitar with a band for years, backing up artists like

Percy Sledge, the Drifters and others. In fact, as part of the inauguration festivities, Lee held a R&B concert featuring such artists as B.B. King, Chuck Jackson, and Carla Thomas—this led to a successful blues album which featured Lee and several of the same artists).

I took the stage and again charged up the crowd. When Vice-President Bush finally made his way to the stage, the crowd was cheering him wildly. He shook my hand on three separate occasions to thank me before he began his talk. Backstage one of his campaign managers pulled me aside to ask about my interest in going on the road with the campaign to emcee similar events. I appreciated the interest, but circumstances and timing would not have allowed me to be away so long.

The next day the media greatly exaggerated the crowd size, and I feel sure that the enthusiasm and noise level contributed to this impression. The Vice President went on to sweep Super Tuesday the following week, and I can't help but feel that the momentum for that victory and his going on to win the Presidency may have begun at the University of South Carolina at Spartanburg that Thursday evening.

After both victorious runs for the governorship, I was requested by Governor Campbell's people to assist in contracting some R&B and beach music entertainment for the inauguration galas. The entertainment at the governor's inaugural ball in 1987 starred the Four Tops and opened with the beach music group the Fantastic Shakers. In 1991, he had the Spinners and beach music's Second Nature. Whenever an opportunity presents itself for the Governor to promote America's golden music, he grabs it.

Governor Campbell has a sterling reputation in the Republican party nationwide, and is well recognized as one of the most successful governors in the country. Mike told me that his father was considering a run for the Presidency in 1996. Hm. Think of the possibilities. Wouldn't it be great to have one of America's golden music's biggest fans residing at 1600 Pennsylvania Avenue, Washington, D.C.?

CHAPTER 20

MR. RAINDROPS

It was 1986 and a couple of years since I had seen Glenn Stetson of the Diamonds, so I phoned him to get an update on what he was doing professionally. He mentioned that he had just finished dinner with a guest, Dee Clark. "You mean the Dee Clark? The man who sang 'Raindrops,' and 'Hey Little Girl,' and 'Just Keep It Up,' and 'Nobody But You,' and . . . ?" Glenn answered, "The one and only." It blew me away as Dee had always been one of my favorite singers, and I had no idea what he was doing, or even if he was still alive. Glenn told me that he was busy booking and promoting and that Dee was one of his main acts. Dee then got on the phone and shyly introduced himself.

He related that he was living in Toccoa, Georgia, at the Lone Oak Motel. We made an appointment for him to tape a live radio show with me a couple of weeks later. He arrived for the taping looking very fit, and in front of the microphone his shyness totally disappeared. Dee's stories were delightful and he told them with much clarity, and insightfulness, yet with a great sense of humor.

Dee, grinning, then related a story about the time he met Fats Domino in New Orleans. After a night on the town, Fats suggested that they get something to eat at one of his favorite late night restaurants. Fats ordered two steaks from the waitress—"the usual, and hurry, I'm hungry!" Dee thought it strange, as he generally ordered his own food, but reasoned, "This is New Orleans, and Fats knows what's best." When the waitress returned, she had two steaks, all right, but they were on the same plate. She served the two steaks to Fats, and Fats looked over to Dee and said, "Aren't you hungry?" Dee confessed his erroneous assumption and placed his order after Fats made it clear, "These two

136

steaks are for the Fat Man."

Laughing, Dee continued with his tales, describing how in the 60's he had been on a tour through the deep south with Sam Cooke, Brook Benton, Jimmy Reed and some other artists traveling in a caravan of cars. In Mississippi they were pulled over by two state troopers who accused some of the drivers of following too closely. Sam Cooke was very offended and began talking to the troopers about his legal rights, and getting his lawyer involved. (Sam was adding fuel to the fire under the circumstances for the time and place.)

Much to Dee's chagrin, Jimmy Reed, with a couple of drinks under his belt and smelling like a brewery, strode over to the officers and belted out, "What's happening Captain Boss Man? This is ole 'Ain't That Loving You Baby' Jimmy Reed." Dee dramatized how the troopers stepped back, and the ticket writer stopped in mid-word and asked in awe, "You don't mean Jimmy Reed the blues singer?" He then asked Jimmy for his autograph. Jimmy cheerfully obliged and gave each trooper an autographed photo. The troopers tore up the tickets and meekly requested that the drivers not follow so closely for the rest of their trip through Mississippi, then apologized for stopping them in the first place, and proceeded to shake each entertainer's hand. Dee chuckled as he related, "Classy, sophisticated Sam Cooke almost got the whole group thrown in jail, while my down to earth, juiced up friend Jimmy Reed saved the day, and maybe the tour."

Along with advertising executive Jerry Dubose, I began working with Dee on an image and publicity campaign to help him secure more bookings. He was in great voice, and his performances were snappy, energetic and professional. His career began picking up, and it was really beginning to look rosy for Dee again. Dee had come to visit Jerry and me to work out details for new photos and brochures. We firmed up that he would be appearing at the 1987 "Swingfest" in Lake Lure, N.C. Having also gotten word through an agent that a tentative concert in Philadelphia with Chubby Checker had been confirmed, he excitedly left Jerry's office for his return trip to Toccoa. The fact that there was a driving rainstorm didn't dampen his enthusiasm one iota.

Later that evening Dee called to tell me that he had had an automobile accident on I-85 on his way home, and there was a nasty bump on his head. He assured me that, other than that, he was all right but that his car was pretty badly damaged. Immediately I urged him to go to a doctor for an examination. He told me that Mrs. Roberts, the owner of the motel where he lived in Toccoa, was also trying to get him to do so. Dee's reply was, "It's just a bump on my head, and I'll be okay."

Several days later when the phone rang, it was an obviously upset Irene Roberts. She was a gentle white woman who had virtually adopted Dee into her family. Things were tight financially for Dee, so she let him pay whenever he could.

Mrs. Roberts informed me that Dee had suffered a stroke and was in the intensive care unit in a hospital in Anderson, S.C. She conjectured that the bump on his head may have contributed to the problem. I arrived at the hospital in Anderson the next morning to find Dee lying in intensive care, tubes and monitors everywhere. I knew that he was terrified. He seemed overjoyed to see me and burst into tears, lamenting what would happen to his newly resurging singing career. He asked me to assist him in dealing with the doctors, nurses, and hospital administration, which, of course I agreed to do. And so began a series of everyday visits. A faux pas by an administrator asking how he could pay for his treatment caused Dee some tearful moments, but with the intercession of Clemson University basketball coach Cliff Ellis (a friend and fan of Dee's) that matter was put to rest.

Dee's conditioned improved enough to allow his transfer to the Roger C. Peace Center in Greenville for physical therapy. Both the Anderson hospital and the Peace Center admitted and treated Dee knowing that he had no insurance and took care of him without reservation.

With child-like innocence Dee phoned to tell me that the Peace Center would let him out for a day over the upcoming July 4th holiday, so I invited him to join my family to see the Four Tops in concert at Greenville's annual hot air balloon extravaganza, "Freedom Weekend Aloft." I arranged for Dee to visit with his old friends and had CBS affiliate, WSPA-TV on hand to do a feature about Dee's visit. Reporter Jane Robelot was genuinely moved by the meeting with Dee. Dee beamed appreciatively the entire evening, even when the rain washed out part of the Four Tops' performance.

One of the highlights of Dee's life was a fund-raiser that Jim Davis, Leighton Grantham and I put on for Dee in August, 1987 at the Greenville Memorial Auditorium. Over two thousand screaming fans got their money's worth that evening as Jerry Butler, Fabian, the Clovers, Clarence "Frogman" Henry, the Dells, Bill Pinkney and the Original Drifters, Billy Scott, Frankie Ford, Pookie Hudson of the Spaniels, the Diamonds, Clifford Curry, Marv Johnson, the Shirelles, Lou Christie, James Brown's half brother—Little Royal, the Dynamic Breakers and Marcel Evans converged on Greenville to support their friend.

The concert's finale at 2:00 A.M., was an emotional rendering of the Spaniels' "Goodnight, Sweetheart" with Bill Pinkney singing bass, and Pookie Hudson singing lead. The other entertainers came back out on-stage to join in, and with moist eyes and smiling faces, the concert ended. Les Timms, the auditorium manager, told me afterwards that it was the most incredible show to ever play at the auditorium.

After being discharged from the Peace Center and returning to Toccoa, Dee was besieged with an outpouring of love and support. Cards, flowers, phone calls, gifts, and even cash donations were sent. Many entertainers including Maurice Williams, Joey Dee, Billy Scott, Ray Peterson, Del Shannon, Glenn Stetson, Johnny Thunder, Doris Jackson of the Shirelles, Bo Diddley, songwriter Otis Blackwell and many others assisted Dee either out of their pocket or in other ways. Bill Pinkney even had Dee join the Original Drifters on tour and paid him to sing one song per performance. One of the National Music Foundation co-founders, Dr. Allan Haimes provided free dental work, and his wife Judith provided travel and lodging for him to journey to Tampa for the work. Two brothers in Atlanta, Harold and Andy Anderson, put on a fundraising concert in Atlanta for Dee. His friends were too numerous to mention, and he gained a real appreciation of just how well loved he was.

Dee suffered congestive heart failure incidences as the months wore on after his stroke. As he lay in intensive care in the hospital on one of those occasions, John Summer, a TV reporter from Tampa joined the visiting Marv Johnson and me for a visit. John was doing a feature on the National Music Foundation and artists down on their luck. The hospital gave clearance for John's interview, and its result was one of the most heart-tugging documentaries I have ever seen—as I viewed old TV footage of Dee, Jackie Wilson, Joe Turner, the Coasters, Joey Dee, Marv Johnson and others, then saw Dee lying there saying, "I had a stroke . . . "

People Magazine did a feature on the foundation and Dee was an integral part. He appeared on the "Sally Jessy Raphael Show," on their behalf as well. His plight was becoming known to many.

Throughout 1990 I heard from Dee at least every couple of weeks. Serving as an entertainment consultant to T-Birds, a nightclub chain in Atlanta and Jacksonville, Florida, I arranged for Dee to perform with Carla Thomas, as he attempted a comeback. Occasionally he would travel to Atlanta to catch performances at T-Birds by some of his old friends like Jerry Butler, the Tams and Bill Pinkney and the Original Drifters. I would always introduce Dee to the audience, and without exception he received heartwarming responses.

Dee suffered a great disappointment in the spring of 1990 when a fund-raiser for him in Toccoa failed to materialize. Some friends there had organized it and he asked if I would emcee it for him. It was scheduled for the Baptist Assembly Auditorium in Toccoa, and I joined Dee for an interview about the concert by a Toccoa weekly newspaper reporter at the paper's offices. That's when all hell broke loose. We had referred to the concert as a rock and roll show, yet when it appeared in the paper, the local Baptists reacted as if it were to be a drunken orgy at a house of prostitution. The Baptist Assembly canceled the show rather than face the disgruntled Baptists' wrath. Apparently rock and roll was viewed as the devil's music in Toccoa, Georgia—a fact which readily overshadowed the simple Christian act of helping a person in need.

The last time I saw Dee was on November 13, 1990. He had asked me to emcee a birthday celebration for him at a "country club on a lake near Anderson, S.C." I arrived to find a country and western honky tonk near Lake Hartwell instead. Singer Jimmy Jordan ("Chapel In The Moonlight") and Grace of Dale and Grace ("I'm Leaving It Up To You") performed and led the audience in singing "Happy Birthday" to Dee. Dee made his way on-stage with his trusty walking cane as "Happy Birthday" resounded throughout. Clearly it was a great birthday celebration for Dee Clark. After all he, a black R&B singer, had been saluted by an all-white country and western crowd which packed the house that Tuesday night.

On December 6, 1990 I was in Columbia, S.C. emceeing the Chairmen of the Board and presenting them with an award at a club called Pug's. Unbeknownst to me, Dee had decided at the last minute to drive to Atlanta so that he could fly out the next morning to Los Angeles to support his protégé, Mark Davis, a contestant on the "Star Search" TV show. Had I known what was about to come down I would have not made the trip.

The next morning Dee was found dead in his motel room in Atlanta. Harold Anderson had taken Dee to T-Birds to catch the Tams' performance and told me that Dee had been in great spirits, and had had a good time. He said that Dee had simply died in his sleep. In spite of Dee's fragile health, his death was hard for me to believe. December 7, Pearl Harbor Day, is historically a sad day in the U.S., but it will be even sadder for me. No more will I answer the phone and hear Dee on the other end, "Harry, I've got an idea and I need your help."

Dee's death made national news, and I had a 30-minute telephone conversation with "Entertainment Tonight" reporter Joel Sarnoff for his extensive story on Dee. He was being remembered in death exactly as he dreamed of being remembered while alive.

With Dee's family's okay, the Roberts family and I arranged for a memorial service to be held in Toccoa December 14—the same day as his funeral service in Chicago. It was a depressingly moving service that damp, cold, Friday at Friendship Baptist Church. Not over thirty people were in attendance, and only one member of the news media—a reporter for the Anderson, S.C. **Independent** newspaper. Billy Scott, Harold Anderson, Jim Davis, Leighton Grantham and the entire Roberts family were there, and several of us spoke. Nothing was more difficult for me than to talk to that small gathering that bone-chilling Friday. As I touched upon the totally unselfish, loving nature of the white Roberts family toward this black man that we all loved, it was hard for me to continue. Their caring all but sustained Dee through his years in Toccoa. There was not a dry eye as a friend of Dee's sang one of Dee's favorite hymns, "How Great Thou Art." Mrs. Roberts' son, Jack, and I paid the minister after everyone had left, then we shook hands—knowing that through one friend, Dee Clark, we shared a bond that few people will ever experience.

Still depressed by the sparse turnout in Toccoa the previous day, I got a phone call which lifted my spirits. It was Pookie Hudson of the Spaniels. Pookie informed me that a turn away crowd had attended Dee's services in Chicago. He said the Dells, the Chi-Lites and many other entertainers had attended. Among those who spoke was Dee's old Vee Jay label mate, Jerry Butler. Later I learned that the service was covered by some national media. Dee would have been very proud, and I could visualize his ear-to-ear grin.

On several occasions when I was with Dee, strangers would come up and ask him, "What was your biggest hit record?" Each time he replied, "'Raindrops,' at least this far in my career." Dee Clark lived and died with the eternal hope that the next hit was just around the corner.

CHAPTER 21

THE AMBASSADOR

Little did I know when Jim Prather and I first met Sonny Turner on the streets of Manhattan in 1962 that we would later become good friends, and little did I know just how good Sonny was as an entertainer. All I knew was that he did a dynamite job as the new lead singer of the Platters.

Sonny had secured the Platters' lead spot as the result of a nation-wide search for the best replacement for the legendary Tony Williams. Tony had decided to go for a solo career, and the Platters were left in the lurch. The Platters had been the reigning vocal group in popular music since the mid-50's, so there was a lot on the line with Tony's departure. Very few things in life are any tougher than following in a legend's foot-steps, but that is just what Sonny did, and with much aplomb.

Before Tony left, the Platters' career had been slightly declining, but they were still widely popular. They continued to record until the mid-60's but without their earlier chart successes. With Sonny singing lead they again hit the charts with "I Love You 1000 Times" and "With This Ring" in 1966. These two songs were more up tempo than the Platters' earlier fare. Nonetheless they gave the Platters' career a much needed boost, and they continued to perform extensively with Sonny as their lead singer. In the early 70's Sonny left the Platters to go solo, as it appeared that their best days were behind them. The musical changes of the time left little room for the Platters' style of music. That is when Sonny Turner's strongest talents were revealed-as he developed into a top-flight nightclub act.

I was aware that Sonny was playing clubs in the South, but had not seen him in person during that time. Even Daddy and Betty had seen him perform live at a private Christmas party at a Greenville area country club before I had ever seen him, and raved about what a showman Sonny was. Though I had begun my radio show in 1976, our paths did not cross until 1980 when he was performing at one of South Carolina's top nightclubs, Vince Perone's Forum in Greenville.

I was able to arrange for Sonny to join me as co-host on one of my radio shows. It was to be the first of several times that he was with me in that capacity. From that point on we developed a real friendship and camaraderie. To this day, he calls me "Cousin Harry," and I in turn call him "Cousin Sonny." At the end of that show, I received a phone call from a listener who seemed real hesitant in asking me a question. Finally getting up her nerve, she wanted to know if Sonny and I were really cousins. I replied without hesitation that we were. She stammered and stuttered and finally asked if I were white. I assured her that I was. "Well," she said, "that proves it. I have been telling my husband all throughout your radio show that the Platters were an all white group, and he didn't believe me." Black Sonny and white Harry both shared a big laugh from that call.

Sonny has been one non-wavering supporter of my efforts to give our type of music and its performers the respect that it so deserves. So when the Miller Brewing Company expressed an interest in sponsoring the Rhythm and Blues-Beach Music Hall of Fame (a brainchild of mine), Sonny joined Bill Pinkney, Maurice Williams, Billy Scott, Clifford Curry, Hall of Fame board members, certain city council members, and me at Spartanburg's City Hall chambers in taping a proposal to present to Miller. After the taping Sonny invited all present to his performance that evening at Vince Perone's Forum. Much to my chagrin, disappointment, and embarrassment only record collector Jim Davis, my secretary, Betty Sharpe, my wife, and I from the Hall of Fame board bothered to show up to witness the historical appearance of Sonny, Maurice, Bill, Billy and Clifford performing "Stand By Me" together on the same stage to honor the Rhythm and Blues/Beach Music Hall of Fame. Unbeknownst to me at the time, the other Hall of Fame board members opted to support one of its fellow board members who was doing his weekly DJ stint at a Spartanburg club that same evening; despite the earlier promises at the taping that they would join Sonny and the other entertainers at the Forum. It was a large, enthusiastic crowd that night, but not because of the Hall of Fame board of directors.

They missed one of the best stage shows anytime, anywhere. The reason is simple. Sonny is the consummate showman. He is a charismatic singer, dancer, and comedian, who has a tremendous stage presence and a special rapport with his audience. Yet he does it with approachable warmth, and not with the arrogance so prevalent with many other performers. Every show of Sonny's, that I have seen, ends with the audience calling for more.

Sonny has always been true to his musical roots as he salutes many of the greats of early American R&B and rock and roll, including the Platters and his idol, Jackie Wilson. Even modern day numbers are done in the style and with the feeling of these musical types. He gently pokes fun at artists like Mick Jagger—then goes right back to what he does best, belting out a soulful song in his own inimitable style.

Today Sonny resides in Las Vegas with his wife and manager, Lois. Most of his performing time is spent in Las Vegas, Reno, and Lake Tahoe where he constantly knocks them dead. On several occasions Sonny has been named Nevada's lounge performer of the year. Consistent with the reality of the industry's turning its back on Sonny's type of music, he has been relegated to the secondary venues, the lounges, and not been featured in their main rooms.

When a friend of mine, Bobby Barber, informed me that he was traveling to Vegas to celebrate his birthday, I got on the phone with Sonny to find out if he was performing during Bobby's trip, which he was. I told him about Bobby's visit and asked him to say hello to Bobby. It blew me away when Bobby returned to Atlanta the next week and told me about the trip.

Bobby, his wife, and two other couples attended Sonny's performance at the Aladdin. Not only did Sonny meet Bobby, he also invited everyone to an after show party at Sonny's condominium, at which Sonny was celebrating his own birthday. They were made to feel totally at home, and they really enjoyed themselves. As they prepared to leave, Sonny announced their departure to his guests then walked with Bobby's group to the cab. To top it off, he paid the cab fare and tip for Bobby's group's return trip to the Mirage where they were staying.

Bobby wondered why Sonny was not playing the casino's main room. I told him my theory about Sonny's type of music never having gotten its rightful acceptance and respect. He looked at me and said, "I think you're right, because I saw several main room shows, and Sonny's show was better than any of them."

Sonny Turner continues to perform at a grueling pace, because it is what he most enjoys doing. His show is not to be missed when visiting Las Vegas, Reno or Lake Tahoe. Surely he will soon make the move to performing in the casinos' main rooms and many more fans will have access to his great performances. But when he does, there is one fact of which I am certain, he will be the same warm person and consummate showman that he is now, and will still remain true to his musical roots. He will see to it that America's golden music gets its proper place in the sun, just as he has. That is the promise of Sonny Turner, Mr. Ambassador.

CHAPTER 22

"FROGMAN"

In 1957 I first heard a song recorded in New Orleans by a singer named Clarence Henry: It had that infectious New Orleans sound and beat through and through, but it was also an exceedingly comical record. The song's title was, "Ain't Got No Home," and featured Clarence singing the first verse in his natural voice and the last two verses in the voices of a girl and a frog—and we teenagers loved it! It reached number 20 on the popular chart and much higher on the R&B chart.

Clarence Henry also had a couple of other hits in the 50's, "Troubles, Troubles, Troubles," and "I Found A Home," the latter an answer song to "Ain't Got No Home." But it was not until 1961 that I heard a record by him again, and it was a monster hit by the title of "But I Do"—it reached number 4 on the national pop music chart. He followed that great hit with a version of the old Mills Brothers song, "You Always Hurt The One You Love," which peaked at number 12 on the pop chart that same year. Yet in Greenville, Clarence proved to be extremely popular during the early 60's and scored on the charts with such songs such as "Lonely Street," "Dream Myself A Sweetheart," "Lost Without You," and "Why Can't You." By that time his name had become Clarence "Frogman" Henry because of the funny frog voice in "Ain't Got No Home."

From the time I joined the Air Force until the early 70's I had lost track of Frogman as he had had no nationally charted records. I had heard that he was performing regularly at a nightclub on Bourbon Street in New Orleans' fabled French Quarter.

Then in the summer of 1970 I took a trip to the crescent city. The first place I visited on Bourbon Street featured a singer playing piano and singing Broadway show tunes. It turned out to be Frankie Ford! The same Frankie Ford who had such national hits like "Sea Cruise," "You Talk Too Much" and "Time After Time" only a decade before! It was a jarring reminder of how the artists had been pushed aside. A little disconcerted, I asked a couple of patrons if they had heard of Frogman, and to my surprise, they directed me to a club where he was playing just a couple of blocks away.

As I was entering the club, I noticed a picture of Frogman with the Beatles, who had visited him when they were in New Orleans a few years earlier. The Beatles had even confessed to being Frogman fans. And . . . there behind the piano was the Frogman—singing some of his old hits, and several by other New Orleans type artists, particularly Fats Domino. Frogman sounded much like Fats, and I was eating it up. I had just gone to heaven on Bourbon Street in New Orleans! There were some New Orleans Saints players in the club, and Frogman dished up his version of Rufus Thomas' hit "Do The Funky Chicken" for them, and taught them the dance steps to the song. It was a great evening, but I did not actually talk with Frogman then, other than to say hello.

Again I lost track of Frogman until 1986 when I attended the New Orleans Jazz and Heritage Festival to get some interviews for my syndicated radio show. Frogman was one of the performers, so I positioned myself near the outdoor stage. It was clear just how well loved he was by the overflow crowd that gathered that hot spring afternoon and Frogman was playing it up to the hilt. There were several people in wheelchairs, and they were literally rocking their chairs in time to the music. Frogman, Junior Walker and the All Stars, Frankie Ford (back doing his hits in great style, thank goodness), Irma Thomas, and Fats Domino all performed that afternoon, giving the audience one helluva performance.

I had recently become acquainted with Frankie Ford and his manager Ken Keene, and we had kept a telephone dialogue going during that time. So when I became involved with promoting the benefit concert for Dee Clark in Greenville in 1987, one of the first artists I contacted about performing was Frankie Ford, and he readily agreed. The next day Ken called to say that he had a surprise for us. Clarence "Frogman" Henry had told Ken that he also would like to perform on the concert and it was quickly arranged.

Frankie, Ken, Frogman, and his wife all emerged from the cramped commuter airplane the day before the concert looking dog-tired.

I shuttled them to the Hyatt Regency in Greenville, and told them that we would see them the next afternoon. Frogman seemed very quiet and reserved during the drive to the hotel, but who wouldn't be, in the company of the gregarious character Frankie Ford!

But the next afternoon as many of the other artists were checking into the hotel, a smiling Frogman strolled into the lobby in a jovial mood. Since there was a piano in the hotel lobby, I kiddingly asked Frogman if he would like to play it. To my surprise, he quickly sat down at the keyboard and began to bang out some tunes and sing. Artists like Marv Johnson, Clifford Curry, and others gathered around for a jam session, along with some fans. Luckily, a fan videotaped the impromptu event and it is more than just a memory.

Frogman and Frankie were two of the real hits at the concert that evening and the crowd loved them. Many consider the show's highlight to be when Frogman waved away the members of the back-up band, Rockin' Robin, who thought that his performance was finished. He tore into the piano, performing the barrel house-boogie woogie-like Fats Domino classic, "Please Don't Leave Me," which brought the house down. The next morning I drove Frogman back to the airport, and we have maintained a good friendship since that time.

In 1989 when I moved to Atlanta, I began to listen to the syndicated Rush Limbaugh radio talk show, which was broadcast over WGST-AM in Atlanta. Quickly I learned that Rush featured news topic updates, such as his "Homeless Update." I was blown away when I heard his "Homeless Update" theme song for the first time. It was none other than "Ain't Got No Home," by my buddy Clarence "Frogman" Henry. I called Frogman and asked if he had heard Rush's show. He was aware that Rush was using his song, but was not that familiar with the show itself.

This was the beginning of the revival of Frogman's career. "Ain't Got No Home" proved to be the most popular of Rush's update songs, and Rush made it a point to meet the Frogman. Since then Frogman has performed on one of Rush's videos and one of Rush's cruises. Frogman and I see each other every year when he comes to Atlanta to see his beloved New Orleans Saints football team play the Atlanta Falcons and we talk quite frequently. He told me that Rush is one of the finest people that he has ever met, and has been quite a friend and supporter. In Rush's

New York Times' chart topping book, <u>The Way Things Ought To Be</u>,[36] he mentions Frogman in the section of the book called, "The Limbaugh Lexicon," as follows: "The Frogman: Clarence 'Frogman' Henry, a rock-and-roll legend and personal friend from New Orleans. His song 'Ain't Got No Home' is the theme music that introduces the Homeless Updates."

One time on Rush's show, presidential candidate Pat Buchanan called Limbaugh and requested "Ain't Got No Home." Then he called again the next day after it was played to thank Rush and tell him how much he liked original good-time rock and roll, Clarence "Frogman" Henry, and "Ain't Got No Home." Thanks to Rush Limbaugh, Frogman's career truly has been reborn.

In February of 1991 I placed a phone call to Frogman and could tell that he was not feeling well. He informed me that while performing on a cruise with Rush Limbaugh, the finger tips of both hands began to feel numb and that he was losing a certain amount of feeling in his legs. Frogman gave me Rush's private number, and I called Rush to inform him of Frogman's plight. Rush's friendship was one of the things that helped Frogman get through this crisis. It was discovered that Frogman had a pinched nerve in his neck and had to have surgery to prevent further damage. Another fan and friend, a surgeon in New Orleans, came to Frogman's aid. Frogman, like many entertainers, had no health insurance, so the surgeon agreed to perform the surgery for free. Though the operation was successful, he is not able to play the piano comfortably, and one leg is not back to full strength. His voice, though, has remained strong.

Today he is performing quite often and he tells me that every place he goes people stop him and bombard him with questions about his good friend, Rush Limbaugh. It is obvious that life today is good for Clarence "Frogman" Henry and he is very optimistic about the future. He is once again able to attend all of the New Orleans Saints' home games, and is enthusiastic about the team. We have gotten a little Atlanta Falcons-New Orleans Saints rivalry thing going, and it is always a kick to hear his infectious "hee-hee-hee" on the other end of the line. Music writers note that Clarence "Frogman" Henry is the man who sings like a frog, but to me he is both a musical legend and a friend.

36 Rush Limbaugh, *The Way Things Ought To Be* (New York, 1992). Limbaugh Lexicon
Appendix.

CHAPTER 23

THE FIRST MOTOWN RECORDING ARTIST

1959 was a great year for good-time rock and roll music and R&F in Greenville. One of my favorite songs that spring was "Come To Me." With the constant bass refrain in the background, it reminded me o, Clyde McPhatter's hit a few months earlier, "A Lover's Question." "Come To Me" was Marv Johnson's first hit. It peaked at number 3(nationally, yet it hit number one in Greenville.

That in itself was not a unique fact, but originally it had been on a lesser known label, Tamla—number 101—as the first record released or the label. The song's co-writer with Marv was none other than Berry Gordy, Jr., the founder of the Motown empire. Berry and his Motown labels (Motown, Tamla, Gordy, Soul, etc.) became extraordinarily success- ful shortly afterwards.

While Berry was just getting his start with Marv Johnson and Jackie Wilson, Jackie was already signed to the established Brunswick label (a subsidiary of Decca) so Jackie's songs already had national distri- bution. The same was not true of Marv's Tamla record. Berry simply did not have sufficient funds to distribute the Tamla product so he turned over distribution rights to United Artists. So Marv became a United Artists recording artist, even though Tamla 101 was the first record or any of the labels which are part of Gordy's "Motown" umbrella.

Marv was very successful with United Artists. He had three othe, hits which reached the national "Top 40" charts. "You Got What It Takes" reached number ten in November, 1959. "I Love The Way You Love" reached number nine in March, 1960. Finally, "(You've Got To) Move Two Mountains" reached number twenty in October, 1960. Yet in Greenville all of them reached the top of the charts. His records "All The Love I've

Got," "I'm Comin' Home," "Merry Go Round," "Baby Baby," "Happy Days," "How Can We Tell Him" and "Ain't Gonna Be That Way" were all hits there as well as throughout much of the South. He was a regular fixture on the national R&B charts. He appeared in the rock and roll movie "Teenage Millionaire" in the early 60's. Marv Johnson was an artist of considerable stature early in his career.

In spite of his success, Marv Johnson was not a household name. Most people would answer, "I don't know," when asked who Marv was. But upon hearing an excerpt from "You Got What It Takes," the answer would usually be, "Oh yeah, I remember that record well." It is ironic that Marv's early hit records provided Berry the funds to start his "Hitsville U.S.A." Motown studio in Detroit yet Marv never became a part of Berry Gordy's later successes.

After the early 60's I had no idea what had happened to Marv. I had not heard any new recordings of his, nor had I seen Marv at any live concerts or on any television shows. Record collector friends were equally as puzzled as to what had happened to him. Once in the late 70's I did a radio feature on Marv and called him "the great disappearing act." I assumed that he had either moved out of the country or that he had died, and it hadn't made the news.

When I received a telephone call from long-time R&B radio personality Cornell Blakely in 1984, I was surprised when he told me that he could get Marv Johnson to come to the Carolinas for a concert or nightclub appearance. Cornell had done a few radio projects with me and I had gotten him involved with a concert I had emceed a couple of years earlier. Cornell did deliver; I dialed the number that he gave me, and sure enough the intelligent, articulate voice on the other end belonged to "the great disappearing act," Marv Johnson.

Marv had been wanting to return to the Carolinas, so I arranged for him to come and do an autograph party and sing along with some of his hits at a local nightclub. When he arrived at the bus station, I recognized him immediately. He looked great and had not aged much at all. We were on our way to dinner, when I put on a tape I had made of his hits. Marv began to sing along with "(You've Got To) Move Two Mountains" and sounded exactly as he had on the recording twenty-four years earlier. Marv was one of the few artists that I had met who still sang in the same key as he did in the 50's and 60's.

153

That trip was to be the first of many of Marv's visits to the Carolinas during the 80's. He returned on a couple of occasions for autograph sessions and he performed at "Swingfest" in Lake Lure, N.C., the Dee Clark benefit concert in 1987, and the nationally-televised, "1988 Beach Music Awards Show" held in Raleigh, North Carolina. We had many opportunities to get together and became fast friends. Erin and Harmon, my two older kids, warmed to him, but Anna, the youngest, adopted him as her favorite singer.

I learned that Marv had continued to reside in Detroit but that he had been only a small part of Berry Gordy's Motown recording factory. It seemed that Marv, being a proud man, simply refused to be a "yes" man to Berry Gordy, and went his own way. Yet in our conversations he harbored no bitterness about Berry's success. He was close friends with many of Motown's stars, and his is quite a story in its own right.

Marv was one of Dee Clark's strongest supporters when he suffered health problems. He was always a tireless worker and supporter of the National Music Foundation (it's mission includes educating the public about American music, and providing for the retirement of professionals from the fields of music, radio, and recording, who can't afford to retire on their own.)

Once he asked me if I would run him by a retirement home so he could visit the relative of a Detroit friend. I heard a piano playing as I was waiting, so I walked in to see what was going on. It was Marv on piano, singing to an enthusiastic throng of elderly folks. Marv's surprise visit cheered up the gloomy place that morning. Later that day his visit to his friend, Dee Clark in the intensive care unit spread more much-needed cheer.

Marv's career was on an upswing in the early 90's, and he had reached a level of popularity in Europe, where he performed quite often. He had a couple of newer recordings, and the future was looking rosy for Marv. It was indeed satisfying to watch "the great disappearing act" reappear.

Monday, May 10, 1993 found me at the Atlanta Greyhound Terminal to again greet Marv. He had made a detour on his way to perform at the Drifters' 40th anniversary celebration with his old friend Bill Pinkney, and was in the greatest of spirits. Later that day we went to Toccoa,

Georgia to see Irene Roberts, who had taken care of Dee Clark during his last days. Looking at photos of Dee that she had kept, Marv's eyes became moist. We left talking in glowing praise of this selfless woman.

During the week we attended an Impressions concert and visited with singer Fred Cash in his hotel room, where war stories were swapped. Marv proudly related how well he was received recently in Europe with the Temptations and that his latest album was doing very well there. His voice fell, though as he talked about how ironic it was that he couldn't get it played in the states.

Marv and I visited his stricken friend Curtis Mayfield. The old days lived again as they visited for several hours. Curtis laughed so much that Marv asked him if it hurt to laugh. The smile on Curtis' face answered Marv very succinctly.

That Friday morning we drove to Bill's anniversary celebration and a reception in Columbia at the Governor's Mansion before the concert. The week itself had been extra special for Marv anyway, and he beamed from ear to ear as he talked to other VIP's at the reception. He was absolutely buoyant as we arrived in Sumter and greeted some of the other entertainers. Marv was upbeat and ready for his performance that evening. The star-studded concert line-up also included Maurice Williams and the Zodiacs, William Bell, Johnny Paycheck, the Swanee Quintet, Billy Scott, the Orioles, Ray Peterson, the Tams, and Bill Pinkney and the Original Drifters among others. Marv was going to show the audience of two thousand that he's, "Got What It Takes."

Emceeing his set, I gave Marv a rousing introduction and he bounded onto the stage to a thunderous ovation. He led off his show by singing "Nobody But You," a tribute to Dee Clark. He then demonstrated some 60's dances, to more applause. He finished with his own hit "You Got What It Takes," but without taking his customary bow or giving me the usual "glad hand." I knew immediately that something was wrong. As I glanced to the side of the stage I saw that Marv had sagged into singer Ray Peterson's arms. I got on the mike and called for a doctor to come to the backstage area.

It was quickly determined that he had suffered a stroke. Marv was conscious and aware of what was going on, but was slurring his words slightly and complaining about numbness on his left side. Marv was rushed by ambulance to the nearby Sumter hospital. Every indica-

155

tion was that he would soon be stabilized and there was no need to stop the show.

But Marv's condition took a turn for the worse and by morning we were advised that the prognosis was not good at all. Marv died at 8:30 Sunday morning May 16, 1993, from a cerebral hemorrhage. His personal effects included a few signed photographs and fourteen dollars and some change.

I'm convinced that his last week was one of the happiest in his life and that he died knowing that a better day was dawning for his music. He had brought good cheer to his friend Curtis Mayfield. He brightened up our lives as he had spent the last week of his life with me. Marv proved to everyone in the audience that last Friday evening that he was a real pro.

As I reflected on the bittersweet events, I remembered Ray Peterson telling me that having to sing his hit "Tell Laura I Love Her" was "one of the toughest things that I've ever done, knowing that Marv was stricken." Yet many felt that Ray never sang better than that night. I was deeply touched to learn that Mike Campbell, the governor's son had gone to the hospital and held Marv's hand while a ventilator breathed for a totally unresponsive Marv.

Always philosophical, one of the last things he told me was how great the song "Dixie" was, as he robustly began singing the tune. He added, "I'm a black man speaking. It's a great traditional song. We have got to get along!" Marv's song "You Got What It Takes" spoke volumes about this compassionate man, once known as the "great disappearing act."

CHAPTER 24

GREAT IMPRESSIONS

The year was 1958, I was 16 years old and a real romantic about life in general. After all, I was only one year away from finishing high school and ready to go out and make it big in the world. I had a job I loved, many good friends, and a loving family. I lived in a great city in the greatest country in the world and had a sense that it was the best time in history to be an American. Life was really good for one Harry Turner.

As a romantic, there was nothing that gave me goose bumps any more than lovey-dovey R&B and rock and roll music. The songs were sung with such feeling, it was impossible not to be moved. My friends and I loved the songs by groups like the Platters, the Dells, the Dubs, Little Anthony & the Imperials, the Dan-Leers, the Chantels and the Five Satins among others. But there was one song that year that was extra special. "For Your Precious Love," was sung by a group out of Chicago called Jerry Butler and the Impressions. While Jerry sang and pleaded and the Impressions responded harmoniously in the background, we guys would hold our dance partners a little closer and squeeze just a little tighter.

That was the only song that I remember by the group until a record called "He Will Break Your Heart" was released in 1960 and it was a solo effort by Jerry Butler. I figured that the Impressions had broken up and would probably not be heard from again. But while Jerry continued to release hit records on his own, I heard a haunting song with great harmony called "Gypsy Woman" and the lead singer had a uniquely high tenor voice. It was 1961 and the label listed the singing group as . . . the Impressions! When I heard the next hit record by the Impressions, it became one of my all time favorites, "It's All Right." This new singer, with the unique tenor voice, was Curtis Mayfield. That's when I realized the staying power of the Impressions. Mayfield's laid back, falsetto tenor style and song writing skill were to influence many artists, including Major Lance, the Temptations, the Chi-Lites, Jan Bradley, Gene Chandler, the Delfonics, and the Stylistics.

In the meantime, Jerry Butler's career was shifting into high gear. He continued to churn out the hits throughout the 60's. In the Carolinas he reached near super star status among the burgeoning Carolina beach music crowd in the latter part of the decade. He released an album, "The Ice Man Cometh," and because of his cool, unflappable demeanor, "The Ice Man" has been his nickname ever since. Having emceed Jerry on several occasions, he has always seemed more like a college professor than an entertainer. His hit records are recognizable to millions. He had such hits as "Moon River," "Find Another Girl," "Hey Western Union Man," "Moody Woman," "What's The Use Of Breaking Up," "Make It Easy On Yourself," "Mr. Dream Merchant," "Only The Strong Survive," and with Betty Everett, "Let It Be Me."

"The Ice Man" has continued to record and perform on occasion. However, he has become very active on the Chicago political scene. He has served as a Cook County Commissioner, a post to which he was re-elected by an overwhelming majority. He is very well respected, and it is conjectured that Butler has a strong shot at one day becoming the Mayor of Chicago.

The last time I saw Jerry was in 1990 when I emceed his performance at T-Birds in Atlanta and the club received a call from a celebrity who wanted to come see Jerry's show. Just as his show began, the legendary Gladys Knight quietly entered and was whisked to an out of the way table. Had Jerry not graciously acknowledged Gladys' attendance, she may have remained anonymous. The crowd went wild, but as would be expected of a Jerry Butler crowd, Gladys was left alone to enjoy the remainder of his performance.

The Impressions kept churning out the hits during the 60's that are instantly recognizable to music fans. After "Gypsy Woman," and "It's All Right," they had such hits as "Talking About My Baby," "I'm So Proud," "Keep On Pushing," "Amen," "People Get Ready," and "We're A Winner." Most were penned by Curtis Mayfield. They had several hits after Curtis left to go solo. Songs like "Finally Got Myself Together," "Same Thing It Took," "You Are My Sunshine," "Sooner Or Later," and "Loving Power."

They, along with Jerry Butler and Curtis Mayfield, were inducted into the Rock and Roll Hall of Fame at the Waldorf Astoria in New York in January of 1991. An anthology on the Impressions has been released by MCA Records. They are embarking on tours with Jerry Butler and others and the demand for their talents continues to increase. Today's group consists of original members Fred Cash and Sam Gooden plus newer members Ralph Johnson and Smokey Vandy Hampton. They sound almost exactly today as they always have, and are real professionals.

The public loves the Impressions and their kind of music but some promoters and booking agents still seem to take groups like them for granted. I recently emceed the Impressions before a large Atlanta convention. As Fred, Sam, Ralph, Smokey and I sat around the dressing room talking before their performance, the booking agent entered, looked at them in their street clothes, and demanded, "Are you boys gonna be ready to go on at 9:00?" They answered simply, "No problem." At 9:00 sharp I brought them on and they hit the stage in their tuxedos, and after a rousing performance which left the audience on their feet shouting, "More!" " More!" "More!," they closed out with their anthem, "Amen." I had to smile as I watched the booking agent yelling for more along with the rest of the crowd.

The Impressions still take care of business.

In 1970 Curtis went solo and had a number of hits in the 70's including "Freddie's Dead," and "Superfly," and he continued to write songs as well as movie soundtracks. He has been one of the few artists to bridge the gap from the 50's to today. With real dismay, I watched news coverage of a freak accident in New York City in 1991. Curtis was onstage preparing to perform at an outdoor concert when a strong gust of wind knocked some lighting equipment directly onto him. Curtis suffered paralysis from the neck down.

Marv Johnson introduced me to bed-ridden Curtis at his Atlanta home in the spring of 1993. Marv and Curtis had been close friends and hadn't seen each other in years. It was quite a reunion! I have stayed in touch with Curtis ever since then.

Curtis has not been forgotten by the industry. In the latter part of 1993 he was inducted into the Georgia Music Hall Of Fame. Warner Brothers made the recent announcement of the February, 1994 release of the compilation album "All Men Are Brothers: A Tribute to Curtis Mayfield," featuring Whitney Houston, Eric Clapton Aretha Franklin, Gladys Knight, Steve Winwood, the Isley Brothers, John Cougar Mellencamp, Stevie Wonder, Elton John, Bruce Springsteen, his former group, the Impressions and others performing Mayfield songs. Proceeds will go to Curtis' family and to the Miami Project, a spinal injury clinic.

Curtis has an inner strength that is evident to those around him. His faith remains undaunted. He has written a book of poetry that will soon be published. Because of his commitment to helping others, he has agreed to be a spokesperson for the 1996 Paralympics. Other great things are yet to be seen and heard from Curtis Mayfield, as he "Keeps On Pushing."

CHAPTER 25

THE LAST ORIGINAL DRIFTER

If I were asked, which was the greatest vocal group of all time based on the number of recordings under their name, without hesitation I would give an emphatic answer—the Drifters! The following lists some of the records they made over the years:

"Money Honey"	"Honey Love"
"White Christmas"	"Drip Drop"
"I Gotta Get Myself a Woman"	"Fools Fall In Love"
"Ruby Baby"	"It Was A Tear"
"Adorable"	"Steamboat"
"Moonlight Bay"	"Hypnotized"
"There Goes My Baby"	"Lonely Winds"
"This Magic Moment"	"Baltimore"
"Dance With Me"	"True Love, True Love"
"Save The Last Dance For Me"	"I Count The Tears"
"Some Kind Of Wonderful"	"Oh My Love"
"Please Stay"	"Sweets For My Sweet"
"When My Little Girl Is Smiling"	"One Way Love"
"Up On The Roof"	"Mexican Divorce"
"On Broadway"	"Vaya Con Dios"
"Under The Boardwalk"	"I'll Take You Home"
"I've Got Sand In My Shoes"	"Nobody But Me"
"Saturday Night At The Movies"	"Little Red Book"
"Kissing In The Back Row"	"Do You Have To Go Now"
"Gonna Move Across The River"	"WPLJ"

The Drifters' recordings are so much a part of the fabric of the American music scene that it is almost taken for granted. Yet the influence of their records is limitless. Such artists as James Taylor, Dolly Parton, George Benson, the Temptations, Dion, Elvis Presley, John Cougar Mellencamp, Narvel Felts, Rick James, the DeFranco Family, Jay and the Americans, Bruce Willis, as well as numerous others reveal the Drifters' influence. The Drifters have even made the unseemly transition to "elevator music" as instrumental versions of their songs can be constantly heard everywhere. This only underscores how well integrated into society their music has become.

The Drifters had three lead singers who had hit records as solo artists. The lead singers and some of their hit records are:

Clyde McPhatter:

"A Lover's Question"
"Without Love"
"Lover Please"
"Since You've Been Gone"
"Treasure Of Love"
"Just To Hold My Hand"
"Long Lonely Nights"
"Lovey Dovey"

"Such A Night"
"Seven Days"
"Come What May"
"Ta Ta"
"Just Give Me A Ring"
"Little Bitty Pretty One"
"Thirty Days"
"Rock And Cry"

Bobby Hendricks:

"Itchy Twitchy Feeling"

Ben E. King:

"Stand By Me"
"Spanish Harlem"
"Don't Play That Song"
"Supernatural Thing"

"I Who Have Nothing"
"Amor"
"Tears, Tears, Tears"
"First Taste Of Love"

Clyde McPhatter, with his clear tenor voice, was the original lead singer for the Drifters on such hits as "Money Honey" and "Honey Love," and he shared lead on "White Christmas" with Bill Pinkney. McPhatter sound-alike Bobby Hendricks was the lead voice on "Drip Drop." Ben E. King sang lead on such hits as "There Goes My Baby,"

162

"Dance With Me," "This Magic Moment," and "Save The Last Dance For Me." When McPhatter and King and their influences on other artists are added, the total Drifters' impact on popular music, R&B, "elevator music" and even country and western is immeasurable.

Today, there is only one member of the original Drifters' group that is still living—my friend Bill Pinkney. Bill is the epitome of the word "trooper." Originally from Dalzell, South Carolina, Bill fought at Normandy Beach and the Rhineland in World War II. After the war, he ended up in New York City playing semi-professional baseball before he began singing in a gospel group. While he was in New York City he met another one-time gospel singer named Clyde McPhatter. Clyde, who was from Durham, North Carolina, was singing with a popular R&B group called the Dominoes—of "Sixty Minute Man" fame.

Clyde wanted more of a say in his music, and the Dominoes were controlled by Billy Ward, a stern taskmaster, so Clyde was looking for another direction to take his remarkable voice. He and Bill convinced some fellow gospel singers, including Gerhart and Andrew Thrasher, to join them in forming a new R&B group. They named the group the Drifters and in 1953 recorded their first hit for Atlantic, "Money Honey." It featured Clyde's tenor voice and Bill's distinctive bass/baritone. Clyde left the group to go solo, but Bill remained with the group until the late 50's.

After Clyde left, Bill was the glue that kept the Drifters together throughout the rest of the 50's. During that time Bill discovered one of their lead singers, Johnny Moore ("Fools Fall In Love," "Ruby Baby," "Under The Boardwalk," etc.) singing in a public rest room in an auditorium in Cleveland, Ohio and signed him to the group. Through the many changes in personnel, Bill has been the one constant in keeping the Drifters' name and their original sound alive.

Bill Pinkney was a vital force in forging the sound of the early gospel-influenced Drifters. His deep, rich voice can be heard on such hits as "Money Honey," "Honey Love," "I Gotta Get Myself A Woman," on which Bill shared lead duties with Johnny Moore, "Fools Fall In Love," "Ruby Baby," "Drip Drop," "Steamboat," "Adorable," and "White Christmas." The Drifters' "White Christmas" is reputed to be the second best selling version of the ever-popular Christmas classic, exceeded only by Bing Crosby's original. In their rendition Bill and Clyde swapped lead, and the slightly upbeat "White Christmas" is still a widely popular holiday favorite. In fact, it was included in the soundtrack of the blockbuster 1990 movie "Home Alone."

In 1988, Bill Pinkney and other Drifters members were inducted into the Rock and Roll Hall of Fame. Although Bill is in his sixties he still performs around 200 nights a year. He has slowed down somewhat, and I stress the word, somewhat. He is still the manager and booking agent for his group, Bill Pinkney and the Original Drifters and still sings in almost every show. He may only be on-stage for five or six songs per set, but it is something truly special when he is.

He has an amazing amount of energy and can "hoof it" on-stage with the best of them. There is a certain twinkle in his eyes and beautiful young girls seem perpetually drawn to Bill at his shows. However, he is a task master with his group, and will react angrily when one of the members gets out of line. He demands that they act in a classy manner, but Bill has a great sense of humor coupled with a real dignity and wisdom, all attributable to the broad experiences of his unique life, and his can-do philosophy.

Anyone who wants to witness a performance that genuinely reflects the 50's scene should see Bill Pinkney and the Original Drifters in person. The group does many of the Drifters' old hits, and the voices and soulful feeling of group members Russell Henry, Richard Knight, Chuck Cockerham and Bill are second to none. It's July, and the audience wants "White Christmas?" They've got it true to the original recording.

The traditional close of one of their shows leaves the audience with a generous helping of pure gospel-tinged Americana. With Bill and other group members swapping lead, they break into the strains of "America The Beautiful," "Battle Hymn Of The Republic," or "Amazing Grace." It is the essence of gospel call and shout. The group adds all the church fervor possible, and inevitably the audience rises to its feet to share a lovefest they won't soon forget. When Bill Pinkney quits performing, a musical era will have lost a true pioneer.

Bemis Locklear, a shagging friend, came backstage at one of Bill's concerts in Atlanta a little while back. Bill was standing in the wings analyzing the other members' performance. Bemis, unaware that he was speaking to Bill Pinkney himself, declared, "Boy, that ole Bill sure does move good for his age." He actually was referring to another singer who was on stage. Bill went right along with Bemis, letting him rave on and on. Finally Bemis started to walk away when he asked, "By the way, what's your name?" Bill replied, "I am Bill Pinkney." Red-faced, Bemis apologized profusely while Bill collapsed with laughter. Yet he had given Bill a compliment as Bill was a good bit older than the other singer. Bill and Bemis both have had many a good laugh about it since.

Bill is in the process of writing a book about the true story of the Drifters. His book will detail, among other things, the sham of the numerous bogus Drifters groups who are performing worldwide and how he has received but a fraction of the royalties due him. He plans to describe how the Drifters were fired en masse in the late 50's because they had the "gall" to demand both a say so in their music and an accounting of royalties on their recordings—and were replaced by another recording group named the Five Crowns, featuring Ben E. King and Charlie Thomas, who then changed their name to the Drifters.

A few months back a friend of mine, Frank Suggs came to see one of Bill's shows. Towards the end of the evening, well past midnight, Bill was in rare form and told the audience that he was going to do the rest of the show for his friend Harry Turner. Bill then tore into some Drifter's songs from the early days such as "Ruby Baby," "Drip Drop," "Steamboat," "Honey Love," "Money Honey," and the show-stopping, "White Christmas." The audience went absolutely bananas! Frank turned to me wide-eyed and exclaimed, "This is one of the best shows I've ever seen!" He then asked me why Bill and his group didn't perform more often in Atlanta in the larger venues. My only answer was, "That's just the way it is."

I have been with Bill on many occasions when I would introduce him around and the reaction would be one of childlike joy and excitement, "Can I have your autograph?" One day the public will overcome the mind set that Bill's music is "oldies," and no longer will it be "just the way it is!"

On May 14, 1993 I emceed Bill Pinkney's 40th anniversary celebration along with "Rocking Ray" Gooding from WBT-AM radio in Charlotte, N.C. S.C. Governor Carroll Campbell, Supreme Court Justice Albert Finney, Comptroller General Earle Morris, wrestler Ric Flair, legendary S.C. TV personality Joe Pinner and other VIP's attended. The Governor presented Bill with the prestigious "Order Of The Palmetto," the highest honor which the state can present to a citizen. Despite the concern about Marv's collapse (which was unknown to most of those in the audience), the air seemed electrically charged that night and it was a fitting tribute to the last original Drifter. Before the event, Bill had been hinting about retirement. Afterwards, he confided to me, "Well Harry, it's been some kind of 40 years, guess its time for me to start on 40 more. I got to keep going and stay active." That was some of the most beautiful Drifters' music I ever heard!

CHAPTER 26

Media And Entertainment Industry Hype

The media and entertainment industry have played a large part in shaping the music we hear, even what we think. They have the ability to create markets, make stars and dictate popular culture. Their power is immense. The following stories illustrate just how skewed their mentality is toward America's golden music, its artists, and the times. This is not just a recent phenomenon. Let's go back to 1958.

Chuck Willis
When rock and roll was new, I was still young and felt, as my friends did, that old age was eons away. And we thought rock and roll entertainers would live forever. On April 10, 1958, we young rock and roll fans were a carefree, devil-may-care lot. Why April 10, 1958? Because that was when we fans lost the <u>first</u> rock and roll star, "The King of the Stroll," Chuck Willis. Rock and rollers Buddy Holly, J.P. "The Big Bopper" Richardson and Ritchie Valens did not meet their fate in a plane crash until almost a year later on February 3, 1959.

Chuck had been riding high, with appearances on American Bandstand and Dick Clark's national Saturday night Beech Nut Chewing Gum rock and roll TV show. Chuck was identified with the first rock and roll dance, the stroll, much as Chubby Checker would be later with the twist. He wore a turban, which gave him a unique and impressive appearance. When news of his death was announced, my friends and I at Greenville High were utterly shocked. He appeared so vibrant, and his career seemed to be going strong, even on the upswing! It was hard to comprehend that Chuck Willis could die of ill health. (He died in Atlanta, Georgia of complications from bleeding ulcers.) His hits "C.C. Rider," "It's

167

Too Late," "Betty And Dupree," "Thunder And Lightning," and "Juanita" were some of our favorites. Since he had just appeared on American Bandstand to promote his upcoming release a few days before he died, it was even harder for us to fathom. That record became a two-sided hit, and was one of rock and roll's great ironies with the titles, "What Am I Living For" and "Hang Up My Rock And Roll Shoes." "What Am I Living For" became his biggest hit ever.

Why has Chuck Willis been overlooked as a great rock and roller who died before his time? Perhaps it was because most rock and roll fans were white and Chuck was black, or that he was a little older when he died. Buddy Holly and Ritchie Valens were very young when they were killed, so it probably hit closer to home. But J.P. Richardson, "The Big Bopper," was older as well and his place in history has been far more significant than that of the great "King of the Stroll." Certainly the drama of a plane crash heightened the interest surrounding the deaths of the young rock and rollers and Richardson, while Chuck Willis died a very quiet death. Buddy Holly's career was in a slump, a fact overshadowed by his fiery death. He paid the ultimate price for fame. There have been movies on the lives of both Buddy Holly and Ritchie Valens.

Following are charted records from Billboard's Top 40 chart for Buddy Holly, Ritchie Valens, J.P. Richardson and Chuck Willis from Joel Whitburn's book, The Billboard Book of Top 40 Hits:

Record	Position	# Of Weeks	Chart Date
Buddy Holly[37]			
"Peggy Sue"	3	16	11/11/57
"Rave On"	37	2	06/09/58
"Early In The Morning"	32	4	08/11/58
"It Doesn't Matter Any More"	13	9	03/09/59
Buddy Holly and the Crickets[38]			
"That'll Be The Day"	1	16	08/19/57
"Oh Boy"	10	13	12/02/57
"Maybe Baby"	17	8	03/10/58
"Think It Over"	27	4	08/04/58
Ritchie Valens[39]			
"Donna"	2	18	12/15/58

168

"La Bamba"	22	8	01/19/59
J.P. Richardson[40]			
("The Big Bopper")			
"Chantilly Lace"	6	22	08/04/58
"Big Bopper's Wedding"	38	1	12/22/58
Chuck Willis[41]			
"C.C. Rider"	12	8	05/13/57
"Betty And Dupree"	33	3	03/10/58
"What Am I Living For"	9	17	05/12/58
"Hang Up My Rock & Roll Shoes"	24	2	05/26/58

Chuck Willis was exceeded on the charts only by Buddy Holly with the Crickets; yet he has been eclipsed by all three from the standpoint of lasting fame. Chuck was "The King of the Stroll," yet the Diamonds are erroneously believed to be holders of that title due to their hit, "The Stroll."

The recording and broadcasting industries are highly reflective of the contributions of Buddy Holly, Ritchie Valens, J.P. "The Big Bopper" Richardson and, yes, Chuck Willis. They paved the way for rock and roll to become a vehicle through which future generations of young people could express themselves.

Buddy Holly, the Big Bopper and Ritchie Valens all sang directly to me as they sang to young people everywhere who loved the music of our time. They were high on my personal list. But Chuck Willis will stroll his way through the story of rock and roll with the verve and flair he embraced in his unforgettable music. The King of the Stroll's rock and roll shoes can never be stilled, nor filled.

Brook Benton

During the time I was building my record collection in the 50's, the name Brook Benton stood out to me as a songwriter. Two of his hits were "Looking Back" by Nat King Cole, and "A Lover's Question" by Clyde McPhatter. At the time I placed him in the same class as Otis Blackwell and Lieber and Stoller.

In early 1959, I first heard a song, "It's Just A Matter Of Time," which knocked me out, and it was sung by Brook Benton. It turned out to be the first in a string of hits for the man from Lugoff, South Carolina whose real name was Benjamin Peay. Other hits were "Endlessly," "So Close," "Thank You Pretty Baby," "So Many Ways," "Fools Rush In," "Kiddio," "My True Confession," "Lie To Me," "The Boll Weevil Song," "Think Twice," "Frankie And Johnny," "Hotel Happiness," and "The Same One." And he had two top ten hits with Dinah Washington, "Baby, You've Got What It Takes" and "A Rockin' Good Way." All were from 1959 to 1963.

Since 1963 he had gone without a hit until 1970, when "Rainy Night In Georgia" became a monster hit, in fact, the best remembered of his career. I thought that Brook was again on his way. But an unfortunate incident at a Grammy Awards telecast in the early 70's put his comeback on permanent hold. Brook had apparently gotten tipsy that evening, and flubbed his part in an award presentation. It was the kiss of death for his "resurrected" career. Yet a similar occurrence was the springboard for the career of the rebellious singer Kris Kristoferson, who was stoned on drugs at another awards presentation.

An excerpt from <u>The</u> <u>Nashville</u> <u>Sound:</u> <u>Bright</u> <u>Lights</u> <u>and</u> <u>Country</u> <u>Music</u>[12] by Paul Hemphill explains how the same thing actually helped Johnny Cash's image: "I remember when he got picked up on pills in El Paso and everybody said, (Well, there it goes, the fans will quit him,)' says Opry singer-comic Archie Campbell, 'but, hell, it made a martyr, a hero, out of him.'"

As the years went by, I often wondered what happened to Brook Benton. One night in 1983 I got a call from Archie Bell, who told me that he was doing some recording work in Charlotte, N.C. at the old Arthur Smith studio. He mentioned that some other artists were also recording there, including Brook Benton. Archie invited me to join him at a press party coming up at the studio, at which Brook was to make an appearance and help promote the recording project.

Brook was to sing a song or two for the gathering, and as he made his entrance he looked slightly thinner, but still, much as I had always remembered him. Lo and behold, he sounded just as he did years earlier— fabulous! I secured a promotional appearance commitment from the recording studio manager, Nick Hice for Brook to join me a couple of weeks later.

Brook and Nick arrived on schedule, and we spent most of the day with local media representatives. He joined me at The Charles Lea Center (for the handicapped) and signed autographs and shook hands with both the students and the workers there. This "forgotten" man was fawned over by almost everyone he met that day. Brook told me that since he severed his ties with Cotillion Records in the early 70's other recording companies wouldn't have anything to do with him, telling him that his music had gone out of style. But here he was, having just recorded his first Christmas album, and it was his first released recording in quite a while.

That evening, Brook and Nick joined me at a local club, and brought about fifty copies of his Christmas album. The place was always crowded, but this particular Friday, people were packed in. Brook signed autographs and in less than an hour they had sold the entire stock of albums. Brook agreed to sing one song acappella and, oh, how he sang—beautifully, sweetly, and soulfully—to thunderous applause. Brook beamed with delight. He left an hour later, and that was the last time I ever saw him.

In April 1988, I was doing my live Saturday radio show when I received a phone call from a listener, Mike MacMillan, who told me that he had just heard that Brook Benton was dead. I couldn't believe it, as nothing had come over the wire services at the station. Still, I kept checking, and there was nothing; so I hoped that it was just an unfounded rumor. After the show, I called Ruth Brown in New York, who knew Brook very well. Ruth was terribly upset and confirmed the worst to me. He was buried a week later, but publicity about his career, death, and burial was minimal at best.

How could this great singer have been so forgotten? It seemed as if the saying, "out of sight, out of mind" was so true in Brook's case. Then, not long after, the great Roy Orbison passed away. Yet, the fanfare was unbelievable. I asked myself, "Why for Roy Orbison but not for Brook Benton?"

The answer is all too clear. Roy, through his association with several of "today's" recording stars via "The Willoughbys" album, had re-attained the status of a peer in the eyes of the powerful and influential rock establishment. Brook, on the other hand, was viewed as just another R&B singer who performed pre-British invasion music.

Joel Whitburn's book, **The Billboard Book Of Top 40 Hits 1955 to Present**[43] bears me out, as to the relative equality of Roy's and Brook's careers. Roy had twenty-two charted records, and Brook had twenty-four.

Roy had nine top 10 records, and Brook had eight.

Atlantic Records' 40th Anniversary Celebration
When word reached me about the fortieth anniversary celebration of
Atlantic Records on HBO in May of 1988, I couldn't wait for it to happen. I
would finally get to see a true salute to Atlantic and the pioneers from the
40's, 50's and 60's who made such incredible music. I knew there would be
live performances of many of my favorites, plus film clips and video tape
of deceased artists like Clyde McPhatter, Chuck Willis, Bobby Darin, Joe
Turner, Otis Redding and Ivory Joe Hunter. Also, I envisioned a backup
band featuring some of the original studio musicians from the heyday of
those original recordings. Anticipation was mine!

My excitement quickly soured. Some of the original artists such as
Ruth Brown, Lavern Baker, Carla Thomas, Sam Moore of Sam and Dave,
and Rufus Thomas all made appearances, but they were brief and token at
best. There was a short salute to only two deceased artists, Otis Redding
and Bobby Darin.

My hopes were not totally dashed because there was an announcement about a powerhouse reunion of one of the all-time great singing
groups yet to come. I knew it would be either the Drifters, the Coasters, or
the Clovers, all of whose members had separated. The program went on
with the announcements, "Stay tuned!" Finally "super group" reunion
time had arrived. I fixed a vodka tonic, settled into my chair, and breath-
lessly awaited the group's introduction. In his best grandstanding fashion,
the announcer introduced this earthshaking group. It turned out to be . . .
not the Drifters . . . not the Coasters . . not the Clovers . . . but that legendary "pioneering" group . . . Led Zeppelin!

Led Zeppelin? I had no problem with the Led Zeppelin reunion
being a part of the special, but backstage were four recording members of
the Coasters—Carl Gardner, Cornell Gunther, Billy Guy, and "Dub"
Jones—together for the first time in over twenty-five years. What music
lover can forget their hits like "Charlie Brown," "Searchin'," "Yakety Yak,"
"Along Came Jones," "Little Egypt," "Young Blood," and "Poison Ivy?"
They sang only one song on the televised program "That Is Rock And
Roll," and it was not even one of their biggest hits.

Joel Whitburn's book[44] also reveals that the Coasters had ten Top 40
records and six Top 10 records while Led Zeppelin only had six Top 40

records and one Top 10 record. Their most well-known song "Stairway To Heaven" was an album cut from "Led Zeppelin IV," in 1971. The affront to the Coasters was all but unforgivable. There was a large TV audience who surely would love to have seen the Coasters perform a medley of their hits and would have enjoyed revisiting the beginnings of their music.

This show illustrated the industry's lack of respect for its own roots—those forerunning, pacesetting artists who literally **created** the industry. In a profound display of skewed vision, the producers, and Atlantic Records' principals, opted to largely ignore the true, groundbreaking pioneers.

Why were there mainly young members in the backup band? And why were the only two acknowledged and saluted deceased artists Bobby Darin and Otis Redding? Debbie Gibson and other current artists got more air time than the original artists-no doubt to promote Atlantic's current sales. Even the appearance of the legendary Sam Moore of Sam and Dave was overshadowed by comedian Dan Aykroyd in his copycat "Blues Brothers" persona.

I have spoken with several of the original R&B performers about the program and there is agreement with my observations. Ahmet Ertegun, the founder of Atlantic Records, should never have allowed these slights to occur. They are analogous to a Disney retrospective with little mention of Mickey Mouse or Donald Duck! I sincerely believe that Ertegun still has a deep love for the original artists and their music and will one day reflect on his label's indomitable pioneers and their immeasurable contributions.

Fats Domino-Almost Forgotten

NBC's "Today" program ran a feature called "The Godfathers of Rock and Roll" March 22-25, 1993. On each day's program a legendary pioneer was featured. They were Chuck Berry, Little Richard, Jerry Lee Lewis and Bo Diddley; all favorites of mine, but each is known almost as much for his unique personality as his music. Although he was the biggest record seller of them all, Fats Domino was totally omitted from the feature. For the sake of argument, here is a comparison of Fats and the other four pioneers from **The Billboard Book of TOP 40 HITS 1955 to Present**[45], by Joel Whitburn:

Artist	Top 40 Hits	Top 10 Hits
Chuck Berry[45]	14	7
Little Richard[46]	9	4
Jerry Lee Lewis[47]	6	3
Bo Diddley[48]	1	0
Fats Domino[49]	36	10

One morning I was reading the paper and preparing for a busy day. I was about to put the paper aside when an article caught my attention; it was about the performance of rocker Jimmy Buffett and the difficulties caused by alcohol restriction at the concert's site, Georgia Tech's stadium-Grant Field. Buffett had long been associated with a margarita drinking, hell raising, island vacation crowd, so therein lay the "hook" to the article. What would the fabled "Parrotheads" do? The article continued, " . . . at 6 P.M. there will be sets by R&B star Fats Domino and South African pop singer Johnny Clegg." I was almost knocked out of my chair!

I couldn't believe that the legendary Fats Domino was coming to Atlanta and would be singing "Blueberry Hill," and "I'm Walkin'," and "Ain't It A Shame," and . . . that's the first I had heard about it! I then spotted the ad for the "Primo Parrothead Party" in big letters. "Jimmy Buffett" was in even larger letters. Below in much smaller letters it read, "Johnny Clegg & Savuka—Fats Domino." No!

I thought, "How could this universally loved singer and charter Rock and Roll Hall of Famer, the man who was second only to Elvis Presley in record sales during the 50's—Antoine 'Fats' Domino—be given second class status for this concert to Jimmy Buffett (with only five top 40 hits and one top 10 hit). And who are Johnny Clegg & Savuka anyway?" The next two days I searched the newspapers far and wide for a story about Fats or a review of his performance. I saw <u>nothing</u>. What a telling commentary it is on the marketing of hype over substance and how we in society have fallen for, even accepted it.

1990 Rock and Roll Hall Of Fame

<u>Rolling Stone</u> magazine reported about the 1990 Rock and Roll Hall of Fame inductions in their February 7, 1991 issue with the cover story which reads: "HALL OF FAME-THE BYRDS TOP THE CLASS OF 1990"[50]. The inductees were:

Lavern Baker
The Byrds
John Lee Hooker
Howlin' Wolf
The Impressions
Wilson Pickett
Jimmy Reed
Ike & Tina Turner
Dave Bartholomew (non-performer)
Ralph Bass (non-performer)

Rolling Stone's story gives exaggerated importance to the folk rock group, the Byrds, on the cover and in the lead article's emphasis. Every other inductee sings America's golden music.

Horace Key of the Tams

In 1991, original member Horace Key of Atlanta R&B singing group the Tams, died suddenly of a heart attack. The Tams had a top ten hit in 1963 with "What Kind Of Fool," and are still favorites today. I had called the Atlanta paper about Horace's death, and was bluntly told by the entertainment editor that he simply didn't have time to write an article because he was "too busy chasing Mick Jagger all over town." [Jagger was in Atlanta filming the movie "Free Jack" at the time]. Apparently news about the everyday comings and goings of the arrogant "bad boy" of British rock were more important than the story of the death of an original American singer in his own home town.

Tony Williams of the Platters

Though I had never met Tony Williams, the original lead singer of the Platters, he was a real favorite of mine. During the summer of 1992 Tony passed away. He sang lead on such timeless classics as "Only You," "The Great Pretender," "The Magic Touch," "My Prayer," "Twilight Time," "Enchanted," "I'm Sorry," "Harbor Lights," and "Smoke Gets In Your Eyes." I'm grateful that Millie Russell, manager of the Orioles, called me with the news because I never saw mention of his death in the Atlanta Journal or Constitution. I had to search far and wide for published news about it.

      On the other hand, a couple of years ago the death of Freddy

175

Mercury of Queen garnered headlines, and an AIDS benefit concert in his memory was televised worldwide. The songs on which Tony Williams sang lead are certifiable classics, whereas with the possible exception of "Another One Bites The Dust," who among us remembers on what songs Freddy Mercury sang lead?

Marv Johnson's Death and the media

Attempting to get information about Marv's death to various media, I was met totally with rebuffs. It was my hope that CNN or "Entertainment Tonight" would have a brief feature on Marv's life and career. I explained the following:

> *He was the first Motown recording artist.
> *He had two Top 10 hits and four Top 40 hits.
> *The money made off his hit records helped finance the legendary Motown operation.
> *He had cheered up his paralyzed friend Curtis Mayfield the day before the concert.
> *He suffered a stroke onstage at the Drifters' 40th anniversary show.
> *He collapsed in singer Ray Peterson's arms.
> *South Carolina governor Carroll Campbell rushed backstage to assist.
> *Marv died less than 36 hours later.

Several of the above circumstances could make stories in themselves. My answer from a representative at "Entertainment Tonight" was a resounding, "There's no hook to the story."

A few weeks later "Entertainment Tonight" ran a feature on R&B singer Arthur Alexander ("You Better Move On," "Anna") after his untimely death in Nashville, Tennessee. It was a moving tribute and I was glad to see it, wondering though at the same time why Arthur Alexander was given tribute and not Marv Johnson, when Marv had more hit records. The piece trumpeted loud and clear the fact that the Beatles had recorded a couple of Arthur Alexander's songs—and that's the kind of "hook" that Marv's life, career and death did not have . . .

And the beat goes on . . .

37 Whitburn, p. 138.

38 Ibid., p. 75.
39 Ibid., p. 281.
40 Ibid., p. 36.
41 Ibid., pp. 294-295.
42 Hemphill, p. 98.
43 Whitburn, pp. 35-36, 203-204.
44 Ibid., p. 67., p. 165.
45 Ibid., p. 36.
46 Ibid., p. 169.
47 Ibid., p. 168
48 Ibid., p. 89.
49 Ibid., pp. 91-92.
50 "Hall Of Fame-The Byrds Top The Class Of 1990," *Rolling Stone*, February 7, 1991., p. 49.

CHAPTER 27

A PROPOSAL

Since I heard my first R&B record, "Drinkin' Wine Spo-Dee-O-Dee" at the age of seven, I have been hooked on the music-with its honest, happy sound. Those days are but memories now, but this timeless music will never die, despite attempts by the sagging recording industry, the robotic broadcast industry, and the slanted media to overlook it in favor of rap, hard rock and an increasingly commercialized country and western.

Yet listen to the thousands of radio and television commercials used to promote countless products worth billions in advertising dollars. (See appendix.) Movies are all the more memorable for golden sound-tracks in such popular classics as **American Graffiti, The Big Chill, Stand By Me, The Blues Brothers, Animal House, Dirty Dancing, Great Balls Of Fire, Sea Of Love, Book Of Love, Hair spray, Father Of The Bride, The Buddy Holly Story, American Hot Wax, Ishtar, Pretty Woman, Home Alone, Sister Act, Fried Green Tomatoes, Malcolm X, The Commitments, My Girl, Shag, The Five Heartbeats, My Blue Heaven, Misery, Ghost,** and countless others. The ever popular "Happy Days," "The Wonder Years," and "Murphy Brown" are only a few examples of television shows that rely on this music to give them flavor.

Compact disc sales have sky-rocketed with artists such as the legendary Fats Domino, Elvis Presley, and James Brown. Motown, Stax/Volt, Atlantic and other labels have released best selling musical anthologies. Labels such as Charly, Ace, Edsel, Rhino, and Ripete have re-released CD's, albums, cassettes, and singles containing original material. Malaco, Ichiban, Alligator, Surfside, Ripete, Metro, Ambient Sound, Classic Artists Recordings and other labels are constantly pumping out new material with the original sound.

Various record producers, as well, are creating fresh material with perenially popular artists. Bruce Patch produces Herb Cox and the Cleftones, Rudy West (of the Five Keys), Margo Sylvia and the Tuneweavers, and Richard Blandon and the Dubs. General Norman Johnson produces the Chairmen of the Board, the Showmen, the Cornelius Brothers and Sister Rose, and Joe Pope and the Tams while Charles Wallert produces such artists as O.C. Smith, Chuck Jackson, and Cuba Gooding of the Main Ingredient. Recently the legendary Capricorn recording studio in Macon, Georgia was purchased by Talmadge Stuckey who has established the Phoenix record label for recording America's golden music.

Smokey Robinson, Sonny Turner of the Platters, and Bill Pinkney and the Original Drifters are but a few of the artists who perform in Las Vegas, Reno, Lake Tahoe, and Atlantic City casinos. Fats Domino, Clarence "Frogman" Henry and other artists play to exuberant, overflow crowds at casinos on the Mississippi Gulf coast. Numerous original artists appear at concerts and festivals all over the U.S., such as the world-famous New Orleans Jazz and Heritage Festival which attracts almost half a million happy fans annually.

Not surprisingly, the group Boyz To Men reached number two on the top singles chart recently, with a re-make of the Five Satins' 50's doo-wop classic, "In The Still Of The Night." Michael Bolton received a Grammy for his recording of the Percy Sledge original "When A Man Loves A Woman." With these and other efforts, a new generation of young people is discovering the music!

Strangely, America's golden music is overtly more popular, more appreciated, and more revered overseas than in the U.S. The late Marv Johnson once wistfully told me that on his last European tour with the Temptations he was continually overwhelmed by the fans' enthusiasm, knowledge of the music and deep love for its pioneers.

America's golden music is uniquely American and must be claimed as a part of our rich cultural history. It is as timeless as our souls. Its lyrics speak to us and its beat carries us, lifting our spirits, enriching our lives and the lives of future generations. In a troubled world, this incredible music, thanks to its creators, has the power to bring us closer together, crossing boundaries that separate and divide.

To my readers I propose this toast: to life, to love, to music, to many magic moments!

COMMERCIALS

These are songs that have been used by companies for national and regional commercials (in some cases, international) over the last several years. These companies, being bottom line conscious, have benefited from the use of America's golden music, or there would not be such an abundance of these types of commercials. There is, however, an obvious dichotomy as to the music's popularity and marketability on the part of the recording and broadcast industries. The recording industry all but ignores it, and the broadcast industry limits this music to week-end and odd hour time slots. Even oldies radio formats feature a predominance of British influenced rock oldies over America's golden music.

ABC Television Network-"ABC"
AT&T-"Dedicated To The One I Love"
AT&T-"I'll Be Around"
AT&T-"Think"
America West-"Respect"
American Express-"I'm In Love Again"
American Express-"Stand By Me"
American Greeting Cards-"Why Do Fools Fall In Love"
Anheuser-Busch-"Stand By Me"
Autolite-"I Got You (I Feel Good)"
Baby Magic Oil-"Slippin' And Slidin'"
Barnett Bank of Florida-"Earth Angel"
Bell South Mobility-"Ain't No Mountain High Enough"
Bic Pens-"Soul Man"
Bon Bon Fruit Scoops-"Tutti-Frutti"
British Airways-"Up On The Roof"
"Brooklyn Bridge" TV Show-"In The Still Of The Night"
Bryant Heat Pumps-"Rescue Me"
Budweiser-"I Love Beach Music"

180

Buick-"Oh Boy"
Burger King-"Great Balls Of Fire"
Burger King-"Whole Lotta Shakin' Going On"
California Raisin Board-"I Heard It Through The Grapevine"
Certs-"Only You"
Chanel Number 5-"Sea Of Love"
Chevrolet-"Personality"
Chevrolet (Chevy City)-"Kansas City"
Chicago Tribune Want Ads-"Get A Job"
Chico-San Rice Cakes-"Summertime, Summertime"
Chunky-"My Boyfriend's Back"
Coca-Cola-"The Twist"
Coppertone-"Yakety Yak"
Dairy Association-"Whole Lotta Shakin' Going On"
Deer Foam Slippers-"Betty Lou Got A New Pair Of Shoes"
Diet Pepsi-"Just One Look"
Dingo Boots-"I'm Walkin'"
Dodge-"The Little Ole Lady From Pasadena"
Doubletree Hotels-"My Boyfriend's Back"
Liquid Drano-"Splish Splash"
Duncan Hines-"I Can't Help Myself"
Eckerds Drugs-"Rockin' Around The Christmas Tree"
Energizer Batteries-"Da Do Ron Ron"
Fantastik-"It's So Easy"
Florists Association-"Just One Look"
Fram-"Who Do You Love?"
Fresh Start Laundry Detergent-"High Heel Sneakers"
GTE-"Splish Splash"
Hardee's-"The Twist"
Head And Shoulders-"Put Your Head On My Shoulders"
Hellman's Dijonnaise-"Duke Of Earl"
Hi-C-"He's So Fine"
Hi-C-"I Wonder Why"
Hi-C-"Little Darlin'"
Hi-C-"Summertime Blues"
Hyatt Hotels-"The Magic Touch"
Hyundai-"Blueberry Hill"
Hyundai-"No Particular Place To Go"
Hyundai-"Stand By Me"
Hyundai-"Whole Lotta Shakin' Going On"
Jaguar-"At Last"
Jewelers Association-"For Your Love"
Jim Dandy Dog Food-"Jim Dandy"

K-Mart-"Personality"
Ken-L Ration Dog Food-"Summertime, Summertime"
Kentucky Fried Chicken-"Come Go With Me"
Kentucky Fried Chicken-"Little Bitty Pretty One"
Kentucky Fried Chicken-"Little Darlin'"
Light And Elegant Diet Food-"Personality"
Little Caesar's Pizza-"Louie, Louie"
Long John Silver's-"Land Of 1000 Dances"
Love Me Tender Dog Chunks-"Love Me Tender"
Dolly Madison Cupcakes-"Good Golly Miss Molly"
Master Card-"My Girl"
Mazda-"Summertime, Summertime"
McDonald's-"Hello Stranger"
McDonald's-"Mack The Knife"
McDonald's-"Shake Rattle And Roll"
McDonald's-"Summertime, Summertime"
Mercury Automobiles-"Be My Baby"
Mercury Automobiles-"Chantilly Lace"
Mercury Automobiles-"Do You Wanna Dance"
Mercury Automobiles-"Mama Said"
Mercury Automobiles-"Reach Out I'll Be There"
Miller Brewing Company-"Think"
Miller Genuine Draft-"I'm A Man"
Miller Genuine Draft-"Mustang Sally"
Miller Lite-"I Like It Like That"
NBC-TV-"Summertime Blues"
Nair-"Short Shorts"
Nabisco-"Barbara Ann"
Nestle's Toll House Cookies-"Summertime Blues"
New Trail Granola Bars-"Goodnight Sweetheart Goodnight"
Nintendo-"The Bird's The Word"
Nintendo-"Witch Doctor"
No Nonsense Panty Hose-"Big Girls Don't Cry"
Nurf-"Surfin' U.S.A."
Nutri-Grain Cereal-"Dedicated To The One I Love"
Ohio Amusement Park-"Summertime Blues"
Oldsmobile-"The Wanderer"
Olympic Fitness Center-"Rock Around The Clock"
Oreo Cookies-"Be My Baby"
Pop Secret Popcorn-"La Bamba"
Pert Plus-"Big Girls Don't Cry"
Peter Pan Peanut Butter-"Peanut Butter"
Pizza Hut-"Rescue Me"

182

Polaroid Camera-"Shout"
Purina Cat Chow-"Calendar Girl"
Quaker Chewy Granola-"Surfin' U.S.A."
Quaker Granola Dips-"Get A Job"
Quaker Peanut Whip Granola Bars-"The Loco-Motion"
Quaker Rice Cakes-"Bread And Butter"
RCA-"I Can See Clearly Now"
Radio Shack-"He's Got The Whole World In His Hands"
Red Lobster-"Only You"
Scott Tissue-"Let The Good Times Roll"
Seagram's Cooler-"This Magic Moment"
Shield Soap-"Rock Around The Clock"
Shout Stain Remover-"Shout"
Six Flags Over Georgia-"Shout"
Skil Power Screw Driver-"The Twist"
Smooshies Toy-"At The Hop"
Sokonol-"I Got You (I Feel Good)"
Southern Bell-"Hold On I'm Comin'"
Southern Bell Yellow Pages-"Just One Look"
Sprint-"Don't Hang Up"
Stouffer's Lean Cuisine-"When A Man Loves A Woman"
Stri-dex Acme Medication-"Wipe Out"
Subaru-"La Bamba"
Subaru-"When A Man Loves A Woman"
Subaru-"You Always Hurt The One You Love"
Liquid Sunlight Dish Detergent-"Breathless"
Super Pretzels-"The Twist"
Sylvan Pools-"Summertime, Summertime"
Teddy Graham Cereal-"Teddy Bear"
Tequila Wine Cooler-"Tequila"
Tone Soap-"Oh Pretty Woman"
Tony's Pizza-"Little Bitty Pretty One"
Toyota-"I'm So Excited"
Toyota-"It's So Easy"
Toyota-"Just One Look"
Turner Broadcasting-"At The Hop"
U.S. Post Office-"What A Difference A Day Makes"
Unisom-"Tossin' And Turnin'"
United Parcel Service-"Be-Bop-A-Lula"
Liquid Vanish-"Duke Of Earl"
Visa (Citibank)-"Stand By Me"
Volvo-"You're The Devil In Disguise"
Water Pik-"What'd I Say"

"Wheel Of Fortune" TV Show-"I'm A Girl Watcher"
"Win, Lose, Or Draw" TV Show-"Shout"

BIBLIOGRAPHY

Barry, Dave. "Play some oldies, but don't turn my stomach." Atlanta *Constitution*. August 23, 1992. B1.

Clark, Dick and Robinson, Richard. *Rock, Roll & Remember*. New York. Thomas Y. Crowell Co., 1976.

Dannen, Fredric. *Hit Men*. New York. Times Books a division of Random House, 1990.

Escott, Colin. *Good Rockin' Tonight*. New York. St. Martin's Press, 1991.

Francis, Connie. *Who's Sorry Now?* New York. St. Martin's Press, 1984.

Gaines, Steven. *Heroes & Villains*. New York. NAL Books, 1986.

George, Nelson. *The Death Of Rhythm & Blues*. New York. Pantheon, 1988.

Goldman, Albert. *The Lives Of John Lennon*. New York. William Morrow And Company, Inc., 1988.

Goldman, Albert. *Sound Bites*. New York. Turtle Bay Books-Random House, 1992.

Gunther, Marc and Carter, Bill. *Monday Night Mayhem*. New York. Beech Tree Books/William Morrow, 1988.

Hemphill, Paul. *The Nashville Sound: Bright Lights and Country Music*. New York. Simon And Schuster, 1970.

Hotchner, A.E. *Blown Away*. New York. Simon And Schuster, 1990.

Jackson, John. *Big Beat Heat*. New York. Schirmer Books, A Division of Macmillan, Inc., 1991.

Jubera, Drew. "Can it Be? Paul Turns 50." Atlanta *Constitution*. June 18, 1992. F4.

Ladd, Jim. *Radio Waves*. New York. St. Martin's Press, 1991.

Limbaugh, Rush. *The Way Things Ought To Be*. New York. Simon And Schuster, 1992.

Marcus, Greil. *Dead Elvis*. New York. Doubleday, 1991.

Phillips, Michelle. *California Dreamin'*. New York. Warner Books, 1986.

Staff Report. "Hall Of Fame-The Byrds Top The Class Of 1990." *Rolling Stone,* Issue 597 (February 7, 1991). p. 49.

Staff and Wire Reports. "Mick Jagger On His Life As a Rocker." Atlanta *Journal-Constitution*. November 14, 1989. L1.

Szatmary, David. *Rockin' In Time*. Englewood Cliffs, N.J. Prentice Hall, 1987.

Thomson, Elizabeth and Gutman, David. *Lennon Companion*. New York. Schirmer Books, 1987.

Welding, Pete and Brown, Toby. *Bluesland*. New York. Penguin Group, 1991.

Whitburn, Joel. *The Billboard Book of Top 40 Hits 1955 to Present*. New York. Billboard Publications, Inc., 1983.

Williams, Otis with Romanowski, Paricia. *Temptations*. New York. G.P. Putman's Sons. 1988.

Wilson, Mary. *Dreamgirl*. New York. St. Martin's Press, 1986.

SUGGESTED READING

Aquila, Richard. *That Old Time Rock & Roll*. New York. Schirmer Books a division of Macmillan, Inc., 1989.

Bego, Mark. *Aretha Franklin, The Queen of Soul*. New York. St. Martin's Press, 1990.

Bronson, Fred. *The Billboard Book of Number One Hits*. New York. Billboard Publications, Inc., 1985.

Brown, Peter and Gaines, Steven. *The Love You Make, An Insider's View of the Beatles*. New York. McGraw-Hill, 1985.

Bugliosi, Vincent with Gentry, Curt. *Helter Skelter*. New York. W.W. Norton & Company, 1974.

Clayson, Alan. *Only The Lonely*. New York. St. Martin's Press, 1989.

Elliott, Marc. *Rockonomics*. New York. Franklin Watts, 1989.

Gray, Andy. *Great Pop Stars*. London, New York, Sidney, Toronto. The Hamlyn Publishing Group Ltd., 1973.

Gregory, Hugh. *Soul Music*. London. Blandford Books, 1991.

Guralnik, Peter. *Sweet Soul Music*. New York. Harper And Row, 1986.

Hampton, Lionel with Haskins, James. *Hamp*. New York. Warner Books, 1989.

Lewis, Peter. *The Fifties*. New York. J.B. Lippincott Company, 1978.

Marcus, Greil. *Mystery Train*. New York. E.P. Dutton & Co., 1975.

Marsh, Dave. *The Heart of Rock and Soul*. New York. A Plume Book, New American Library, 1989.

Medved, Michael. *Hollywood Vs. America*. New York. Harper Collins, 1992.

Millar, Bill. *The Drifters*. New York. The Macmillan Company, 1971.

Miller, Jim, Kingsbury, Robert. *The Rolling Stone Illustrated History of Rock & Roll*. New York. Rolling Stone Press, Random House, 1976.

Nite, Norm N. *Rock On*. New York. Thomas Y. Crowell Co., 1974.

Presley, Patricia Beaulieu with Harmon, Sandra. *Elvis and Me*. New York. G.P. Putnam's Sons, 1985.

Reeves, Richard. *A Question of Character*. Rocklin, Ca. Prima Publishing, 1992.

Robinson, Smokey with Ritz, David. *Smokey-Inside My Life*. New York. McGraw-Hill, 1989.

Sanjek, Russell, Sanjek, David. *American Popular Music Business in the 20th Century*. New York, Oxford. Oxford University Press, 1991 .

Santelli, Robert. *Sixties Rock-A Listener's Guide*. Chicago. Contemporary, 1985.

Shore, Michael with Clark, Dick. *The History of American Bandstand*. New York. Ballantine Books, 1985.

Singleton, Ranoma Berry. *Berry, Me, and Motown*. Chicago. Contemporary, 1990.

Smith, Joe. *Off The Record*. New York. Warner Books, 1988.

Smith, Wes. *The Pied Pipers of Rock and Roll*. Marietta, Ga. Longstreet Press, 1989.

Tataborelli, J. Randy. *Call Her Miss Ross*. New York. Birch Lane Press; Carol Publishing Group, 1989.

Tosches, Nick. *Unsung Heroes of Rock 'n' Roll*. New York, Harmony Books, 1984.

Wade, Dorothy and Picard. *Music Man*. New York, London, W.W. Norton & Company, 1990.

Ward, Ed, Stokes, Geoffrey, Tucker, Ken. *Rock Of Ages*. New York. Rolling Stone Press/Summit Books, 1986.

Wyman, Bill with Coleman, Ray. *Stone Alone*. New York. Vikinq Penguin. 1990.

INDEX

191

194